# Company's Coming®

# 150 Delicious Squares

Jean Paré

www.companyscoming.com
visit our website

## Divider Photo

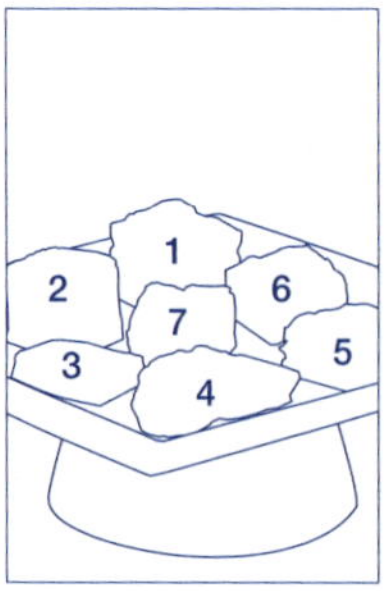


1. Nutty Spice Slice, page 58
2. Marshmallow Squares, page 46
3. Peanut Butter Bars, page 82
4. Chocolate TV Roll, page 21
5. Gumdrop Bars, page 79
6. Cream Cheese Brownies, page 80
7. Bikini Bars, page 133

Props courtesy of:
Cherison Enterprises Inc.

*We gratefully acknowledge the following suppliers for their generous support of our Test and Photography Kitchens:*

*Broil King Barbecues*
*Corelle®*
*Hamilton Beach® Canada*
*Lagostina®*
*Proctor Silex® Canada*
*Tupperware®*

# Get more great recipes...FREE!

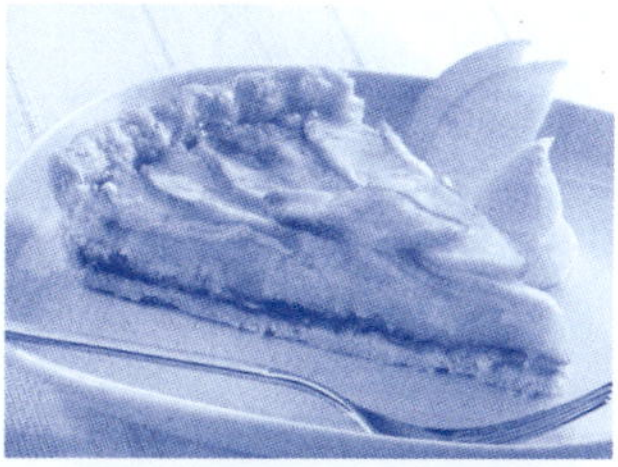

click

search

print

cook

From apple pie to zucchini bread, we've got you covered. Browse our free online recipes for Guaranteed Great!™ results.

You can also sign up to receive our **FREE online newsletter**. You'll receive exclusive offers, FREE recipes & cooking tips, new title previews, and much more...all delivered to your in-box.

So don't delay, visit our website today!

**www.companyscoming.com**

visit our website

# Table of Contents




Tips for Cutting and Storing Squares

Unbaked Squares

Baked Squares


# *Dedication*

*Special thanks to my mother, Ruby Elford, from whom I learned to appreciate good cooking. Also dedicated to my father, Edward Elford, who praised even my earliest attempts.*

# Foreword

For almost as long as I can remember, I have been compiling recipes in boxes, scrap books, files and more boxes. Through years of catering, I used most of the recipes in this book at one function or another, many of which have been requested by those attending.

Every recipe in this book has been tried and taste-tested many times. Make some squares. Brew some coffee. Call your friends. Company's coming!

*Jean Paré*

### Nutrition Information Guidelines

Each recipe is analyzed using the most current version of the Canadian Nutrient File from Health Canada, which is based on the United States Department of Agriculture (USDA) Nutrient Database.

- If more than one ingredient is listed (such as "butter or hard margarine"), or if a range is given (1 – 2 tsp., 5 – 10 mL), only the first ingredient or first amount is analyzed.
- For meat, poultry and fish, the serving size per person is based on the recommended 4 oz. (113 g) uncooked weight (without bone), which is 2 – 3 oz. (57 – 85 g) cooked weight (without bone)—approximately the size of a deck of playing cards.
- Milk used is 1% M.F. (milk fat), unless otherwise stated.
- Cooking oil used is canola oil, unless otherwise stated.
- Ingredients indicating "sprinkle," "optional," or "for garnish" are not included in the nutrition information.
- The fat in recipes and combination foods can vary greatly depending on the sources and types of fats used in each specific ingredient. For these reasons, the amount of saturated, monounsaturated and polyunsaturated fats may not add up to the total fat content.

Vera C. Mazurak, Ph.D.
Nutritionist

# Tips for Cutting and Storing Squares

## Cutting

The first step in being able to cut perfect squares is to line the pan with foil. Once the squares have been thoroughly chilled or baked and cooled, you can remove them from the pan. Simply lift them out by holding the edges of the foil and place them on a cutting surface. For a 9 x 9 inch (22 x 22 cm) pan, use a long, sharp knife to cut the square in half. Be sure to clean the knife between every cut. Press straight down through the centre of each half, and cut in half again. Working on one quarter at a time, cut each section into three strips. Then turn and make three cuts the other way. Each section yields nine squares, making a total of 36 for the whole pan. An 8 x 8 inch (20 x 20 cm) pan may be cut into 36 squares if it is a rich recipe. Otherwise, you may have to use a ruler to cut 5 by 5 pieces to make 25.

To cut through a top chocolate or meringue layer, heat the knife in hot water. If cutting through chocolate, dry the knife quickly with a paper towel and press down slowly so the chocolate softens slightly as you make the cut. If cutting through meringue, leave the knife wet. Clean the knife in hot water and repeat for each cut.

## Storing

You may freeze each recipe very successfully. If iced, squares can be stored in the freezer for up to one month. If they're un-iced, they can be kept frozen longer. All the icings can be made and frozen in separate containers. Be sure to allow icing to reach room temperature before using. If more liquid is needed, it may be added then. When added before room temperature is reached, icing will be runny when it warms.

Keep unbaked squares covered and chilled until ready to serve—especially on hot days.

# Peanut Butter Crispy Squares

*Definitely a favourite among the kids, but we all eat and enjoy them.*

| | | |
|---|---|---|
| **Sweetened condensed milk** | **2/3 cup** | **150 mL** |
| **Brown sugar, packed** | **1/2 cup** | **125 mL** |
| **Corn syrup** | **1/4 cup** | **60 mL** |
| **Smooth peanut butter** | **1/4 cup** | **60 mL** |
| **Crisp rice cereal** | **4 cups** | **1 L** |
| **TOPPING** | | |
| **Semi-sweet chocolate chips** | **1/2 cup** | **125 mL** |
| **Smooth peanut butter** | **2 tbsp.** | **30 mL** |

Combine first 4 ingredients in large saucepan. Heat and stir on low until melted and thickened. Remove from heat.

Add cereal. Stir until coated. Press firmly into greased 9 x 9 inch (22 x 22 cm) pan. Let stand until set.

**Topping:** Heat chocolate chips and peanut butter in small saucepan on lowest heat, stirring often, until chocolate is almost melted. Remove from heat. Stir until smooth. Spread evenly over cereal layer. Cuts into 36 squares.

***1 square:*** *76 Calories; 3 g Total Fat (0.2 Mono, trace Poly, 1.0 g Sat); 1 mg Cholesterol; 13 g Carbohydrate; trace Fibre; 1 g Protein; 52 mg Sodium*

Pictured on page 17.

# Crispy Rice Squares

*A simple, classic treat that gets eaten as quickly as it's made.*

| | | |
|---|---|---|
| **Butter (or hard margarine)** | **1/4 cup** | **60 mL** |
| **Large marshmallows** | **32** | **32** |
| **Crisp rice cereal** | **5 cups** | **1.25 L** |

Heat butter and marshmallows in large heavy saucepan on low, stirring constantly, until melted. Remove from heat.

Add cereal. Stir until coated. Press firmly into greased 8 x 8 inch (20 x 20 cm) pan (see Note). Let stand in pan on wire rack until set. Cuts into 25 squares.

*(continued on next page)*

*1 square: 60 Calories; 1.9 g Total Fat (0.5 g Mono, 0.1 g Poly, 1.2 g Sat); 5 mg Cholesterol; 10 g Carbohydrate; trace Fibre; 1 g Protein; 71 mg Sodium*

Pictured on page 17.

**CHOCOLATE CRISPY RICE SQUARES:** Heat 3 tbsp. (50 mL) butter (or hard margarine) and 1 cup (250 mL) semi-sweet chocolate chips in small, heavy saucepan on lowest heat, stirring often, until almost melted. Remove from heat. Stir until smooth. Spread evenly over squares.

**Note:** You can also use an 9 x 9 (22 x 22 cm) pan for this recipe.

# Chocolate Roll

*This colourful confection freezes well. Cut a few slices, then pop the rest back in the refrigerator or freezer.*

| | | |
|---|---|---|
| **Semi-sweet chocolate chips** | **1 cup** | **250 mL** |
| **Butter (or hard margarine)** | **2 tbsp.** | **30 mL** |
| **Large egg, fork-beaten (see Safety Tip)** | **1** | **1** |
| **Miniature multi-coloured marshmallows** | **2 1/2 cups** | **625 mL** |
| **Icing (confectioner's) sugar** | **1 cup** | **250 mL** |
| **Chopped walnuts** | **1/2 cup** | **125 mL** |
| **Quartered maraschino cherries, well drained** | **1/2 cup** | **125 mL** |
| **Medium unsweetened coconut** | **1/2 cup** | **125 mL** |

Heat chocolate chips and butter in large heavy saucepan on lowest heat, stirring often, until almost melted. Remove from heat. Stir until smooth.

Add egg. Mix well. Stir in next 4 ingredients until coated. Roll mixture into 12 inch (30 cm) long log.

Sprinkle coconut evenly over sheet of waxed paper, slightly longer than log. Roll log in coconut until coated. Wrap with plastic wrap. Chill for about 2 hours until firm. Cut into 1/4 inch (6 mm) slices. Makes about 48 slices.

*1 slice: 59 Calories; 2.8 g Total Fat (0.6 g Mono, 0.7 g Poly, 1.4 g Sat); 6 mg Cholesterol; 8 g Carbohydrate; trace Fibre; trace Protein; 9 mg Sodium*

Pictured on page 17.

**Safety Tip:** This recipe contains uncooked egg. Make sure to use fresh, clean Grade A eggs. Keep chilled. Pregnant women, young children or the elderly are not advised to eat anything containing raw egg.

# Chocolate Crisps

*Anyone at any age can make this in a flash. It's like candy to eat.*

| | | |
|---|---|---|
| **Liquid honey** | **3/4 cup** | **175 mL** |
| **Smooth peanut butter** | **1 cup** | **250 mL** |
| **Semi-sweet chocolate chips** | **1 cup** | **250 mL** |
| **Salted peanuts** | **1 cup** | **250 mL** |
| **Crisp rice cereal** | **3 cups** | **750 mL** |

Combine honey and peanut butter in small, heavy saucepan. Bring to a boil on low, stirring constantly. Remove from heat.

Add chocolate chips. Stir until melted.

Add peanuts and cereal. Stir until coated. Press firmly into greased 9 x 9 inch (22 x 22 cm) pan. Chill until set. Cuts into 36 squares.

***1 square:** 125 Calories; 7.6 g Total Fat (0.5 g Mono, 0.1 g Poly, 2.2 g Sat); 0 mg Cholesterol; 13 g Carbohydrate; 1 g Fibre; 3 g Protein; 81 mg Sodium*

Pictured on page 17.

# Coconut Roll

*A slice of heaven for coconut lovers.*

| | | |
|---|---|---|
| **Fine coconut** | **1 1/2 cups** | **375 mL** |
| **Smooth peanut butter** | **1/2 cup** | **125 mL** |
| **Corn syrup** | **3 tbsp.** | **50 mL** |
| **Fine coconut** | **1/4 cup** | **60 mL** |

Mix first 3 ingredients in medium bowl until combined. Roll into 8 inch (20 cm) long log, about 1 1/2 inches (3.8 cm) in diameter.

Sprinkle second amount of coconut evenly over sheet of waxed paper, slightly longer than log. Roll log in coconut until coated. Wrap with plastic wrap. Chill for about 3 hours until firm. Cut into 1/4 inch (6 mm) slices, using serrated knife. Makes about 30 slices.

***1 slice:** 59 Calories; 5.0 g Total Fat (0.1 g Mono, trace Poly, 2.9 g Sat); 0 mg Cholesterol; 3 g Carbohydrate; 1 g Fibre; 1 g Protein; 23 mg Sodium*

Pictured on page 17.

# Fancy Whip Up

*A pretty and tasty treat that's very easy to make. Store in refrigerator until needed.*

| | | |
|---|---|---|
| Whole graham crackers | 9 | 9 |
| Large egg (see Safety Tip) | 1 | 1 |
| Icing (confectioner's) sugar | 1 1/2 cups | 375 mL |
| Butter (or hard margarine), softened | 1/2 cup | 125 mL |
| Vanilla extract | 3/4 tsp. | 4 mL |
| Salt, sprinkle | | |
| Medium unsweetened coconut | 1 cup | 250 mL |
| Chopped maraschino cherries, well drained | 1/2 cup | 125 mL |
| Chopped walnuts | 1/2 cup | 125 mL |
| Whole graham crackers | 9 | 9 |
| ICING | | |
| Icing (confectioner's) sugar | 1 1/2 cups | 375 mL |
| Butter (or hard margarine), softened | 3 tbsp. | 50 mL |
| Water | 1 1/2 tbsp. | 25 mL |
| Vanilla extract | 1/2 tsp. | 2 mL |

Line bottom of ungreased 8 x 8 inch (20 x 20 cm) pan with first amount of graham crackers, trimming to fit.

Beat next 5 ingredients in medium bowl until thick and smooth.

Add next 3 ingredients. Mix well. Spread evenly over crackers in pan.

Cover with second amount of graham crackers trimmed to fit .

**Icing:** Beat all 4 ingredients in small bowl until smooth, adding more water or icing sugar as necessary until spreading consistency. Spread evenly over graham crackers. Chill for about 4 hours until crackers start to soften. Cuts into 25 squares.

***1 square:*** *158 Calories; 9.0 g Total Fat (1.7 g Mono, 1.4 g Poly, 5.2 g Sat); 22 mg Cholesterol; 19 g Carbohydrate; 1 g Fibre; 1 g Protein; 54 mg Sodium*

Pictured on page 17.

**Safety Tip:** This recipe contains uncooked egg. Make sure to use fresh, clean Grade A eggs. Keep chilled. Pregnant women, young children or the elderly are not advised to eat anything containing raw egg.

# Midnight Mints

*The perfect ending to lunch or supper—the minty taste goes with just about anything. Store in refrigerator or freezer.*

| | | |
|---|---|---|
| **BOTTOM LAYER** | | |
| Butter (or hard margarine) | 1/2 cup | 125 mL |
| Cocoa, sifted if lumpy | 1/3 cup | 75 mL |
| Granulated sugar | 1/4 cup | 60 mL |
| Large egg, fork-beaten (see Safety Tip) | 1 | 1 |
| Graham cracker crumbs | 1 3/4 cups | 425 mL |
| Fine coconut | 3/4 cup | 175 mL |
| Finely chopped walnuts | 1/2 cup | 125 mL |
| **MINT LAYER** | | |
| Icing (confectioner's) sugar | 2 cups | 500 mL |
| Butter (or hard margarine), softened | 1/3 cup | 75 mL |
| Milk | 3 tbsp. | 50 mL |
| Peppermint extract | 1 tsp. | 5 mL |
| Drop of green liquid food colouring | 1 | 1 |
| **CHOCOLATE LAYER** | | |
| Semi-sweet chocolate chips | 2/3 cup | 150 mL |
| Butter (or hard margarine) | 2 tbsp. | 30 mL |

**Bottom Layer:** Heat first 3 ingredients in medium saucepan on low, stirring often, until sugar is dissolved. Stir in egg until thickened. Remove from heat.

Add next 3 ingredients. Mix well. Press firmly into greased 9 x 9 inch (22 x 22 cm) pan.

**Mint Layer:** Beat first 4 ingredients in medium bowl until smooth, adding more milk or icing sugar as necessary until spreading consistency. Add food colouring. Beat well. Spread evenly over bottom layer. Chill for about 2 hours until set.

**Chocolate Layer:** Heat chocolate chips and butter in small, heavy saucepan on lowest heat, stirring often, until chocolate is almost melted. Remove from heat. Stir until smooth. Let stand until lukewarm. When cool but still runny, spread evenly over mint layer. Chill for about 30 minutes, until set. Cuts into 36 squares.

*(continued on next page)*

*1 square: 133 Calories; 8.5 g Total Fat (1.9 g Mono, 1.2 g Poly, 4.7 g Sat); 19 mg Cholesterol; 14 g Carbohydrate; 1 g Fibre; 1 g Protein; 63 mg Sodium*

Pictured on page 17 and on back cover.

**Safety Tip:** This recipe contains uncooked egg. Make sure to use fresh, clean Grade A eggs. Keep chilled or frozen. Pregnant women, young children or the elderly are not advised to eat anything containing raw egg.

# Baba Rum Roll

*A variation of the Eastern European favourite. Apricot jam replaces the traditional use of raisins, giving this roll some extra sweetness.*

| | | |
|---|---|---|
| **Finely crushed vanilla wafers (about 96) (see Note)** | **3 cups** | **750 mL** |
| **Cocoa, sifted if lumpy** | **3 tbsp.** | **50 mL** |
| **Apricot jam** | **1/4 cup** | **60 mL** |
| **Dark (navy) rum** | **3 tbsp.** | **50 mL** |
| **Water** | **1/4 cup** | **60 mL** |
| **Apricot jam** | **1 tbsp.** | **15 mL** |
| **Water** | **2 tsp.** | **10 mL** |
| **Chocolate sprinkles** | **1/3 cup** | **75 mL** |

Combine wafer crumbs and cocoa in medium bowl. Add first amount of jam and rum. Stir well. Add first amount of water, 1 tbsp. (15 mL) at a time, mixing well after each addition until mixture holds together when pressed. Divide mixture in half. Roll each half into 6 inch (15 cm) long log, about 1 1/2 inches (3.8 cm) in diameter.

Combine second amounts of jam and water. Brush over logs.

Sprinkle chocolate sprinkles evenly over sheet of waxed paper, slightly longer than logs. Roll each log in sprinkles until coated. Let stand, uncovered, at room temperature for about 2 hours until dry. Cut into 1/4 inch (6 mm) slices. Makes about 48 slices.

*1 slice: 66 Calories; 1.9 g Total Fat (0 g Mono, 0 g Poly, 0.6 g Sat); 2 mg Cholesterol; 11 g Carbohydrate; trace Fibre; 1 g Protein; 54 mg Sodium*

Pictured on page 17.

**Note:** This is equal to approximately one 11 oz. (312 g) box of vanilla wafers.

# Favourite Butterscotch Squares

*Be sure to try this—it's sure to please.*

| | | |
|---|---|---|
| Whole graham crackers | 12 – 13 | 12 – 13 |
| Butter (or hard margarine) | 3/4 cup | 175 mL |
| Brown sugar, packed | 2/3 cup | 150 mL |
| Milk | 1/2 cup | 125 mL |
| Vanilla extract | 1 tsp. | 5 mL |
| Graham cracker crumbs | 1 1/4 cups | 300 mL |
| Whole graham crackers | 12 – 13 | 12 – 13 |
| ICING | | |
| Icing (confectioner's) sugar | 1 1/2 cups | 375 mL |
| Butter (or hard margarine), softened | 3 tbsp. | 50 mL |
| Water | 4 tsp. | 20 mL |
| Vanilla extract | 1/2 tsp. | 2 mL |

Line ungreased 9 x 9 inch (22 x 22 cm) pan with first amount of graham crackers, cutting to fit. Set aside.

Combine next 4 ingredients in large saucepan. Bring to a boil on medium, stirring often. Reduce heat to medium-low. Simmer for 5 minutes. Remove from heat.

Add graham crumbs. Stir. Pour over crackers in pan.

Cover with second amount of graham crackers, cutting to fit. Let stand in pan on wire rack until cool.

**Icing:** Beat all 4 ingredients in small bowl until smooth, adding more water or icing sugar as necessary until spreading consistency. Spread evenly over graham crackers. Let stand, covered, for at least 6 hours or overnight until crackers are softened. Cuts into 36 squares.

***1 square:*** *102 Calories; 5.4 g Total Fat (1.5 g Mono, 0.4 g Poly, 3.2 g Sat); 13 mg Cholesterol; 13 g Carbohydrate; trace Fibre; 1 g Protein; 68 mg Sodium*

Pictured on page 17.

# Cereal Squares

*This sweet spin turns breakfast cereal into an after-dinner dessert.*

| | | |
|---|---|---|
| **Brown sugar, packed** | **1/2 cup** | **125 mL** |
| **Corn syrup** | **1/2 cup** | **125 mL** |
| **Smooth peanut butter** | **1/2 cup** | **125 mL** |
| **Cornflakes cereal, lightly packed** | **2 cups** | **500 mL** |
| **Crisp rice cereal** | **1 cup** | **250 mL** |
| **ICING** | | |
| **Brown sugar, packed** | **1/2 cup** | **125 mL** |
| **Butter (or hard margarine)** | **1/4 cup** | **60 mL** |
| **Half-and-half cream** | **2 tbsp.** | **30 mL** |
| **Icing (confectioner's) sugar** | **1 cup** | **250 mL** |

Combine brown sugar and corn syrup in large saucepan. Heat and stir on medium until sugar is dissolved. Remove from heat. Add peanut butter. Stir until smooth.

Add both cereals. Stir until coated. Press firmly into greased 9 x 9 inch (22 x 22 cm) pan. Let stand until set.

**Icing:** Combine first 3 ingredients in small saucepan. Heat and stir on medium until melted. Bring to a boil. Reduce heat to medium-low. Simmer, uncovered, for 1 minute, stirring occasionally. Transfer to medium bowl. Cool for about 30 minutes until lukewarm.

Add icing sugar. Beat until light and creamy, adding more cream or icing sugar as necessary until spreading consistency. Spread evenly over cereal layer. Cuts into 36 squares.

***1 square:*** *91 Calories; 3.3 g Total Fat (0.4 g Mono, trace Poly, 1.3 g Sat); 4 mg Cholesterol; 16 g Carbohydrate; trace Fibre; 1 g Protein; 49 mg Sodium*

Pictured on page 17.

### Paré Pointer

*The best time to sample all the goodies you want is when you are so tired or so busy that you will forget you had any—your body can't remember if your brain forgets.*

# Truffle Slices

*A snap to make. The smooth, creamy texture melts in your mouth. Best to chill before serving.*

| | | |
|---|---|---|
| **Butter (or hard margarine), softened** | **1/2 cup** | **125 mL** |
| **Cocoa, sifted if lumpy** | **1/3 cup** | **75 mL** |
| **Icing (confectioner's) sugar, sifted** | **1 1/2 cups** | **375 mL** |
| **Ground walnuts (or pecans)** | **1/2 cup** | **125 mL** |

Beat butter and cocoa in medium bowl until smooth. Add icing sugar. Mix well. Roll into 7 inch (18 cm) long log, about 1 1/2 inches (3.8 cm) in diameter.

Sprinkle walnuts evenly over sheet of waxed paper, slightly longer than log. Roll log in walnuts until coated. Wrap with plastic wrap. Chill for 1 hour. Cut into 1/4 inch (6 mm) slices. Makes about 28 slices.

***1 slice:*** *69 Calories; 4 g Total Fat (1.0 g Mono, 0.9 g Poly, 2.2 g Sat); 9 mg Cholesterol; 7 g Carbohydrate; trace Fibre; trace Protein; 23 mg Sodium*

Pictured on page 18.

# S'mores

*Just like the campfire variety, but these can be made all year long. Mmmm, s'more please!*

| | | |
|---|---|---|
| **Whole graham crackers** | **8** | **8** |
| **Squares of milk chocolate bar (two 1 1/2 oz., 45 g, bars)** | **16** | **16** |
| **Large marshmallows** | **4** | **4** |

Place 4 graham crackers on broiler pan. Arrange 4 squares of chocolate over each graham cracker. Arrange marshmallows over chocolate. Broil on centre rack in oven for about 1 minute until marshmallows are golden. Immediately press remaining graham crackers over marshmallows. Cool slightly. Makes 4 s'mores.

***1 s'more:*** *171 Calories; 8.0 g Total Fat (0.4 g Mono, 0.3 g Poly, 4.6 g Sat); 5 mg Cholesterol; 24 g Carbohydrate; 1 g Fibre; 2 g Protein; 60 mg Sodium*

Pictured on page 17.

*(continued on next page)*

**Variation:** Try using your favourite flavoured chocolate bars to personalize your s'mores. Mint chocolate works particularly well.

# Saucepan Brownies

*At last, a brownie you can make on a day that's too hot to think about cooking—no oven needed for this one. It has an exceptionally rich chocolate flavour.*

| | | |
|---|---|---|
| **Semi-sweet chocolate chips** | **2 2/3 cups** | **650 mL** |
| **Evaporated milk (or half-and-half cream)** | **1 cup** | **250 mL** |
| **Finely crushed vanilla wafers (about 96), see Note** | **3 cups** | **750 mL** |
| **Miniature marshmallows** | **2 cups** | **500 mL** |
| **Chopped walnuts** | **1 cup** | **250 mL** |
| **Icing (confectioner's) sugar** | **1 cup** | **250 mL** |
| **Salt** | **1/2 tsp.** | **2 mL** |
| **Evaporated milk (or half-and-half cream)** | **2 tsp.** | **10 mL** |

Heat chocolate chips and first amount of evaporated milk in saucepan on medium-low, stirring often, until chocolate is almost melted. Remove from heat. Stir until smooth. Reserve 1/2 cup (125 mL) in small bowl.

Add next 5 ingredients to saucepan. Mix well. Press firmly into greased 9 x 9 inch (22 x 22 cm) pan.

Stir second amount of evaporated milk into reserved chocolate mixture. Spread evenly over brownie layer. Chill until set. Cuts into 36 squares.

***1 square:*** *182 Calories; 8.5 g Total Fat (1.6 g Mono, 1.7 g Poly, 3.3 g Sat); 5 mg Cholesterol; 26 g Carbohydrate; 1 g Fibre; 3 g Protein; 112 mg Sodium*

Pictured on page 18.

**Note:** This is equal to approximately one 11 ounce (312 gram) box of vanilla wafers.

### *Paré Pointer*

*While attending a convention, this is your chance to consume all kinds of extras. After all, it is a professional obligation, not food intake.*

# Jellied Marshmallows

*A clever little recipe that will bring "How did you do that?" from everyone. Keep chilled until just before serving.*

**Cooking spray**

| | | |
|---|---|---|
| **Box of jelly powder (gelatin), any flavour** | **3 oz.** | **85 g** |
| **Boiling water** | **2/3 cup** | **150 mL** |
| **Granulated sugar** | **1 cup** | **250 mL** |
| **Light corn syrup** | **3 tbsp.** | **50 mL** |
| **Icing (confectioner's) sugar** | **1/3 cup** | **75 mL** |

Line 8 x 8 inch (20 x 20 cm) pan with foil. Spray with cooking spray.

Combine jelly powder and boiling water in small saucepan. Heat and stir on medium-low until dissolved. Add granulated sugar. Stir until dissolved. Add corn syrup. Stir well. Transfer to large bowl. Chill, uncovered, for about 40 minutes, stirring every 10 minutes and scraping down sides, until very thick and almost, but not quite, set. Beat for about 10 minutes, until smooth. Pour into prepared pan. Spread evenly. Chill, uncovered, for at least 6 hours or overnight.

Sift half of icing sugar onto large sheet of waxed paper. Invert gelatin mixture onto icing sugar. Remove foil. Dust with remaining icing sugar. Cut into squares, dusting each with icing sugar until coated. Makes about 25 marshmallows.

***1 marshmallow:*** *54 Calories; trace Total Fat (0 g Mono, 0 g Poly, 0 g Sat); 0 mg Cholesterol; 11 g Carbohydrate; 0 g Fibre; 3 g Protein; 8 mg Sodium*

Pictured on page 35.

1. S'mores, page 14
2. Chocolate Roll, page 7
3. Midnight Mints, page 10
4. Crispy Rice Squares, page 6
5. Coconut Roll, page 8
6. Peanut Butter Crispy Squares, page 6
7. Cereal Squares, page 13
8. Chocolate Crisps, page 8
9. Favourite Butterscotch Squares, page 12
10. Baba Rum Roll, page 11
11. Fancy Whip Up, page 9

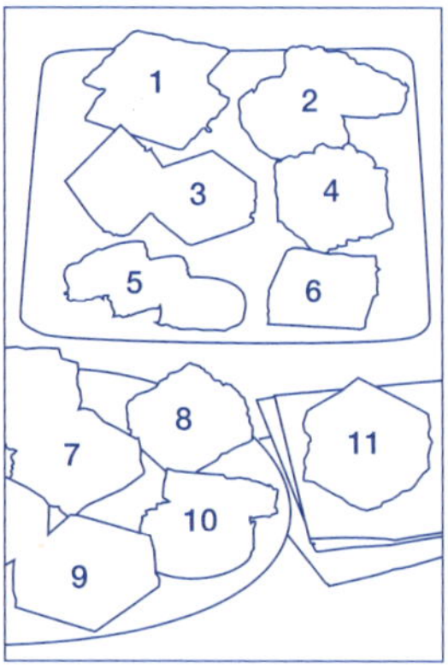

# Chocolate Coconut Layer

*A good contrast of light and dark layers. Chocolate really completes the taste.*

| | | |
|---|---|---|
| **Egg whites (large), fork-beaten (see Safety Tip)** | **3** | **3** |
| **Icing (confectioner's) sugar** | **5 1/4 cups** | **1.3 L** |
| **Medium unsweetened coconut** | **3 3/4 cups** | **925 mL** |
| **Vanilla extract** | **3/4 tsp.** | **4 mL** |
| **Butter (or hard margarine)** | **3/4 cup** | **175 mL** |
| **Cocoa, sifted if lumpy** | **2 tbsp.** | **30 mL** |

Mix first 4 ingredients in large bowl.

Heat butter in small saucepan on medium until melted. Let stand for 5 minutes to cool. Add to coconut mixture. Mix well. Spread half of mixture evenly in greased 8 x 8 inch (20 x 20 cm) pan. Smooth top.

Add cocoa to remaining coconut mixture. Mix well. Press firmly over bottom layer. Chill for about 1 hour until firm. Cuts into 36 squares.

***1 square:*** *155 Calories; 8.8 g Total Fat (1.2 g Mono, 0.2 g Poly, 6.8 g Sat); 10 mg Cholesterol; 19 g Carbohydrate; 1 g Fibre; 1 g Protein; 35 mg Sodium*

Pictured on page 35.

**Safety Tip:** This recipe contains uncooked egg. Make sure to use fresh, clean Grade A eggs. Keep chilled. Pregnant women, young children or the elderly are not advised to eat anything containing raw egg.

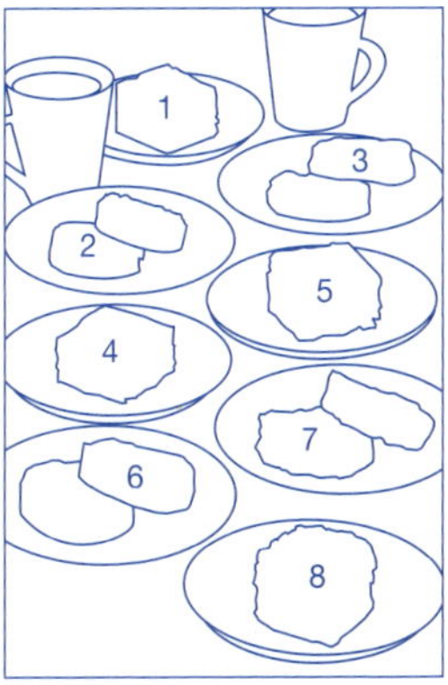


1. Saucepan Brownies, page 15
2. Apricot Roll, page 20
3. Graham Mint Roll, page 20
4. Chocolate Boil, page 22
5. Raisin Quickie, page 24
6. Fruit Roll, page 22
7. Truffle Slices, page 14
8. Fudgy Macaroons, page 29

# Graham Mint Roll

*These can also be shaped into tiny balls to serve as an after-lunch mint substitute.*

| | | |
|---|---|---|
| **English mints (about 35)** | **1/2 cup** | **125 mL** |
| **Graham cracker crumbs** | **2 cups** | **500 mL** |
| **Can of sweetened condensed milk** | **11 oz.** | **300 mL** |
| **Medium unsweetened coconut** | **1/2 cup** | **125 mL** |
| **Medium unsweetened coconut** | **1/3 cup** | **75 mL** |

Process mints in blender until fine crumbs form. Transfer to medium bowl. Add next 3 ingredients. Stir well. Let stand for about 10 minutes, until crumbs are softened. Divide mixture in half. Roll each half into 6 inch (15 cm) long log, about 2 inches (5 cm) in diameter.

Sprinkle second amount of coconut evenly over sheet of waxed paper, slightly longer than logs. Roll each log in coconut until coated. Wrap each log with plastic wrap. Chill for about 3 hours until firm. Cut into 1/4 inch (6 mm) slices. Makes about 48 slices.

***1 slice:** 54 Calories; 1.6 g Total Fat (0.2 g Mono, 0.1 g Poly, 1.0 g Sat); 2 mg Cholesterol; 9 g Carbohydrate; trace Fibre; 1 g Protein; 29 mg Sodium*

Pictured on page 18.

# Apricot Roll

*Subtle, natural sugars help to sweeten this fruity roll.*

| | | |
|---|---|---|
| **Finely chopped, dried apricot** | **1 cup** | **250 mL** |
| **Finely crushed vanilla wafers (about 24 wafers)** | **3/4 cup** | **175 mL** |
| **Finely chopped pitted dates** | **1/2 cup** | **125 mL** |
| **Medium unsweetened coconut** | **1/2 cup** | **125 mL** |
| **Icing (confectioner's) sugar** | **1/3 cup** | **75 mL** |
| **Grated lemon zest** | **2 tsp.** | **10 mL** |
| **Orange juice, approximately** | **3 tbsp.** | **50 mL** |
| **Brandy extract** | **2 tsp.** | **10 mL** |
| **Granulated sugar** | **2 tbsp.** | **30 mL** |

*(continued on next page)*

Combine first 6 ingredients in large bowl.

Combine orange juice and extract in small cup. Drizzle over fruit mixture. Mix until crumbs are moistened. Roll into 9 inch (22 cm) long log, about 1 1/2 inches (3.8 cm) in diameter.

Sprinkle sugar evenly over sheet of waxed paper, slightly longer than log. Roll log in sugar until coated. Wrap with plastic wrap. Chill for about 2 hours until firm. Cut into 1/4 inch (6 mm) slices. Makes about 36 slices.

*__1 slice:__ 53 Calories; 2.0 g Total Fat (trace Mono, trace Poly, 0.9 g Sat); 0 mg Cholesterol; 9 g Carbohydrate; 1 g Fibre; trace Protein; 8 mg Sodium*

Pictured on page 18.

# Chocolate TV Roll

*This variation of the Chocolate Roll uses cocoa instead of chocolate chips, and has graham cracker crumbs that give it more texture.*

| | | |
|---|---|---|
| **Large egg, fork-beaten (see Safety Tip)** | **1** | **1** |
| **Miniature multi-coloured marshmallows** | **2 cups** | **500 mL** |
| **Icing (confectioner's) sugar** | **1 cup** | **250 mL** |
| **Chopped walnuts** | **1/2 cup** | **125 mL** |
| **Cocoa, sifted if lumpy** | **1/2 cup** | **125 mL** |
| **Graham cracker crumbs** | **1/2 cup** | **125 mL** |
| **Butter (or hard margarine), melted** | **2 tbsp.** | **30 mL** |
| **Medium unsweetened coconut** | **1/2 cup** | **125 mL** |

Combine first 7 ingredients in large bowl until all are moistened. Roll mixture into 12 inch (30 cm) long log.

Sprinkle coconut evenly over sheet of waxed paper, slightly longer than log. Roll log in coconut until coated. Wrap with plastic wrap. Chill for about 2 hours until firm. Cut into 1/4 inch (6 mm) slices. Makes about 48 slices.

*__1 slice:__ 41 Calories; 2.0 g Total Fat (0.3 g Mono, 0.6 g Poly, 0.8 g Sat); 6 mg Cholesterol; 5 g Carbohydrate; trace Fibre; 1 g Protein; 12 mg Sodium*

Pictured on divider page.

**Safety Tip:** This recipe contains uncooked egg. Make sure to use fresh, clean Grade A eggs. Keep chilled. Pregnant women, young children or the elderly are not advised to eat anything containing raw egg.

# Fruit Roll

*The sweetness of this roll comes mostly from the fruit.*

| | | |
|---|---|---|
| Chopped pitted dates | 1/2 cup | 125 mL |
| Chopped red glazed cherries | 1/2 cup | 125 mL |
| Raisins (or currants) | 1/2 cup | 125 mL |
| Chopped glazed pineapple | 1/4 cup | 60 mL |
| Chopped walnuts | 1/4 cup | 60 mL |
| Medium unsweetened coconut | 1/4 cup | 60 mL |
| Salt | 1/8 tsp. | 0.5 mL |
| Granulated sugar | 2 tbsp. | 30 mL |

Process first 7 ingredients in food processor until finely chopped. Mix well, adding a bit of water if needed to make it cling together. Form into 7 inch (18 cm) long log, about 2 inches (5 cm) in diameter.

Sprinkle sugar evenly over sheet of waxed paper, slightly longer than log. Roll log in sugar until coated. Wrap with plastic wrap. Chill for at least 6 hours or overnight. Cut into 1/4 inch (6 mm) slices, using serrated knife. Makes about 28 slices.

***1 slice:*** *48 Calories; 1.1 g Total Fat (0.1 g Mono, 0.5 g Poly, 0.4 g Sat); 0 mg Cholesterol; 10 g Carbohydrate; 1 g Fibre; trace Protein; 15 mg Sodium*

Pictured on page 18.

# Chocolate Boil

*A great time-saving, no-bake, semi-sweet square.*

| | | |
|---|---|---|
| Large eggs, fork-beaten | 2 | 2 |
| Brown sugar, packed | 1 cup | 250 mL |
| Butter (or hard margarine) | 1/2 cup | 125 mL |
| Cocoa, sifted if lumpy | 2 tbsp. | 30 mL |
| Milk | 1 tbsp. | 15 mL |
| Graham cracker crumbs | 3 cups | 750 mL |
| Chopped walnuts | 1/2 cup | 125 mL |
| Medium unsweetened coconut | 1/2 cup | 125 mL |
| Salt | 1/4 tsp. | 1 mL |

*(continued on next page)*

**CHOCOLATE GLAZE**

| | | |
|---|---|---|
| **Semi-sweet chocolate chips** | **1 cup** | **250 mL** |
| **Butter (or hard margarine)** | **2 tbsp.** | **30 mL** |

Combine first 5 ingredients in large saucepan. Bring to a boil on medium, stirring constantly. Boil gently for 1 minute, without stirring. Remove from heat.

Add next 4 ingredients. Stir well. Press firmly into greased 9 x 9 inch (22 x 22 cm) pan. Let stand until set.

**Chocolate Glaze:** Heat chocolate chips and butter in small, heavy saucepan on lowest heat, stirring often, until chocolate is almost melted. Remove from heat. Stir until smooth. Let stand for 5 minutes. Spread evenly over squares. Chill for about 30 minutes, until set. Cuts into 36 squares.

*__1 square:__ 126 Calories; 7.3 g Total Fat (1.8 g Mono, 1.2 g Poly, 3.7 g Sat); 20 mg Cholesterol; 15 g Carbohydrate; 1 g Fibre; 1 g Protein; 88 mg Sodium*

Pictured on page 18.

# Rainbow Pastel

*Coconut lovers will appreciate these colourful bars. They are simple to make and add variety to a tray of goodies. To freeze, wrap airtight to keep them from drying.*

| | | |
|---|---|---|
| **Icing (confectioner's) sugar** | **2 cups** | **500 mL** |
| **Fine coconut** | **4 1/2 cups** | **1.1 L** |
| **Can of sweetened condensed milk** | **11 oz.** | **300 mL** |
| **Drops of red liquid food colouring** | **4** | **4** |
| **Drops of yellow liquid food colouring** | **2** | **2** |
| **Drops of green liquid food colouring** | **2** | **2** |

Combine first 3 ingredients in large bowl. Divide into 3 equal portions.

Add red food colouring to 1 portion. Mix well. Repeat with remaining portions and food colourings. Press each portion firmly into layers in 8 x 4 inch (20 x 10 cm) ungreased loaf pan. Chill for about 1 hour until set. Cut into 1/2 inch (12 mm) slices. Cut each slice vertically into 4 bars. Makes about 64 bars.

*__1 bar:__ 78 Calories; 5.0 g Total Fat (0.2 g Mono, 0.1 g Poly, 4.3 g Sat); 1 mg Cholesterol; 8 g Carbohydrate; 1 g Fibre; 1 g Protein; 8 mg Sodium*

Pictured on page 35.

# Raisin Quickie

*A rich, caramel taste coats layers of crunchy graham crackers and juicy raisins. Store in refrigerator.*

| | | |
|---|---|---|
| Whole graham crackers | 12 – 13 | 12 – 13 |
| Raisins (or currants) | 3/4 cup | 175 mL |
| Water | 1/4 cup | 60 mL |
| Granulated sugar | 1 cup | 250 mL |
| Butter (or hard margarine) | 1/2 cup | 125 mL |
| Cocoa, sifted if lumpy | 1 tbsp. | 15 mL |
| Large egg, fork-beaten | 1 | 1 |
| Graham cracker crumbs | 1 cup | 250 mL |
| Chopped walnuts | 1/2 cup | 125 mL |
| Whole graham crackers | 12 – 13 | 12 – 13 |
| COFFEE ICING | | |
| Icing (confectioner's) sugar | 1 1/4 cups | 300 mL |
| Cocoa, sifted if lumpy | 1/4 cup | 60 mL |
| Butter (or hard margarine), softened | 3 tbsp. | 50 mL |
| Hot strong prepared coffee | 1 1/2 tbsp. | 25 mL |

Line ungreased 9 x 9 inch (22 x 22 cm) pan with first amount of graham crackers, cutting to fit.

Combine raisins (or currants) and water in medium saucepan. Bring to a boil on medium. Boil gently for 2 minutes. Reduce heat to medium-low.

Add next 4 ingredients. Heat and stir until butter is melted and mixture is slightly thickened. Remove from heat.

Add graham crumbs and walnuts. Stir well. Spread evenly over crackers in pan.

Cover with second amount of graham crackers, cutting to fit.

**Coffee Icing:** Beat all 4 ingredients in medium bowl until smooth, adding more coffee or icing sugar as necessary until spreading consistency. Spread evenly over graham crackers. Chill covered in refrigerator for several hours to soften crackers. Cuts into 36 squares.

***1 square:*** *115 Calories; 5.3 g Total Fat (1.3 g Mono, 1.1 g Poly, 2.5 g Sat); 15 mg Cholesterol; 17 g Carbohydrate; 1 g Fibre; 1 g Protein; 55 mg Sodium*

Pictured on page 18.

# Butterscotch Coconut Squares

*This doesn't require baking and is very tasty. For coconut lovers.*

| | | |
|---|---|---|
| Butterscotch chips | 1/2 cup | 125 mL |
| Butter (or hard margarine) | 1/4 cup | 60 mL |
| Large egg, fork-beaten (see Safety Tip) | 1 | 1 |
| Graham cracker crumbs | 2 cups | 500 mL |
| Medium unsweetened coconut | 1 cup | 250 mL |
| Chopped walnuts | 1/2 cup | 125 mL |
| Vanilla extract | 1 tsp. | 5 mL |
| Salt | 1/4 tsp. | 1 mL |
| VANILLA CUSTARD ICING | | |
| Icing (confectioner's) sugar | 1 cup | 250 mL |
| Butter (or hard margarine), softened | 2 tbsp. | 30 mL |
| Milk | 4 tsp. | 20 mL |
| Vanilla custard powder | 1 tbsp. | 15 mL |
| Vanilla extract | 1/2 tsp. | 2 mL |

Heat butterscotch chips and butter in large heavy saucepan on lowest heat, stirring often, until almost melted. Remove from heat. Stir until smooth.

Add next 6 ingredients. Mix well. Press firmly into greased 9 x 9 inch (22 x 22 cm) pan. Let stand in pan on wire rack until cool.

**Vanilla Custard Icing:** Beat all 5 ingredients in medium bowl until smooth, adding more milk or icing sugar as necessary until spreading consistency. Spread evenly over bottom layer. Chill, covered, for at least 6 hours or overnight. Cuts into 36 squares.

***1 square:*** *96 Calories; 5.8 g Total Fat (0.9 g Mono, 1.1 g Poly, 3.5 g Sat); 11 mg Cholesterol; 10 g Carbohydrate; 1 g Fibre; 1 g Protein; 66 mg Sodium*

Pictured on page 35.

**Safety Tip:** This recipe contains uncooked egg. Make sure to use fresh, clean Grade A eggs. Keep chilled. Pregnant women, young children or the elderly are not advised to eat anything containing raw egg.

**CHOCOLATE COCONUT SQUARES:** Use semi-sweet chocolate chips instead of butterscotch chips.

# Snow Log

*This light-coloured, cherry-flavoured slice makes a good contrast on a tray of chocolate sweets.*

| | | |
|---|---|---|
| **Cream cheese, softened** | **4 oz.** | **125 g** |
| **Icing (confectioner's) sugar** | **1 1/2 cups** | **375 mL** |
| **Finely crushed vanilla wafers (about 40)** | **1 1/4 cups** | **300 mL** |
| **Chopped maraschino cherries, well drained** | **1/2 cup** | **125 mL** |
| **Salt** | **1/4 tsp.** | **1 mL** |
| **Finely crushed vanilla wafers (about 11)** | **1/3 cup** | **75 mL** |

Beat cream cheese and icing sugar in large bowl until smooth. Add next 3 ingredients. Mix well. Work in more icing sugar if needed for firmness. Roll into 9 inch (22 cm) long log, about 1 3/4 inches (4.5 cm) in diameter.

Sprinkle second amount of wafer crumbs evenly over sheet of waxed paper, slightly longer than log. Roll log in crumbs until coated. Wrap with plastic wrap. Chill for about 2 hours until firm. Cut into 1/4 inch (6 mm) slices. Makes about 36 slices.

*1 slice: 70 Calories; 2.1 g Total Fat (0 g Mono, 0 g Poly, 1.0 g Sat); 4 mg Cholesterol; 12 g Carbohydrate; trace Fibre; 1 g Protein; 61 mg Sodium*

Pictured on page 35.

# Bridge Peel Dainties

*You can't guess the taste of these by looking at them—you have to try them.*

| | | |
|---|---|---|
| **Diced mixed peel** | **2 cups** | **500 mL** |
| **Miniature marshmallows** | **2 cups** | **500 mL** |
| **Graham cracker crumbs** | **1 1/2 cups** | **375 mL** |
| **Can of sweetened condensed milk** | **11 oz.** | **300 mL** |
| **Chopped pitted dates** | **1 cup** | **250 mL** |
| **Chopped walnuts** | **1 cup** | **250 mL** |
| **Graham cracker crumbs** | **1/4 cup** | **60 mL** |

Combine first 6 ingredients in large bowl. Mix well. Divide in half. Roll each half into 9 inch (22 cm) log, about 1 1/2 inches (3.8 cm) in diameter.

*(continued on next page)*

Sprinkle second amount of graham crumbs evenly over sheet of waxed paper, slightly longer than log. Roll each log in crumbs until coated. Wrap with plastic wrap. Chill for at least 6 hours or overnight. Cut into 1/4 inch (6 mm) slices, using serrated knife. Makes about 72 slices.

***1 slice:*** *59 Calories; 1.6 g Total Fat (0.2 g Mono, 0.9 g Poly, 0.4 g Sat); 1 mg Cholesterol; 11 g Carbohydrate; 1 g Fibre; 1 g Protein; 23 mg Sodium*

Pictured on page 35.

# TV Roll

*Enjoy this attractive, coloured marshmallow roll while you're watching your favourite TV show.*

| | | |
|---|---|---|
| **Large egg, fork-beaten (see Safety Tip)** | **1** | **1** |
| **Miniature, multi-coloured marshmallows** | **2 cups** | **500 mL** |
| **Brown sugar, packed** | **1 cup** | **250 mL** |
| **Chopped walnuts** | **1/2 cup** | **125 mL** |
| **Graham cracker crumbs** | **1/2 cup** | **125 mL** |
| **Butter (or hard margarine), melted** | **2 tbsp.** | **30 mL** |
| **Shredded coconut** | **1/2 cup** | **125 mL** |
| **Drops of red liquid food colouring** | **2 – 3** | **2 – 3** |

Combine first 6 ingredients in large bowl. Roll mixture into 12 inch (30 cm) long log.

Measure coconut into container with lid. Add food colouring. Shake to distribute food colouring evenly. Sprinkle coconut evenly over sheet of waxed paper, slightly longer than log. Roll log in coconut until coated. Wrap with plastic wrap. Chill for about 2 hours until firm. Cut into 1/4 inch (6 mm) slices. Makes about 48 slices.

***1 slice:*** *45 Calories; 1.8 g Total Fat (0.3 g Mono, 0.6 g Poly, 0.7 g Sat); 6 mg Cholesterol; 7 g Carbohydrate; trace Fibre; trace Protein; 16 mg Sodium*

Pictured on page 36.

**Safety Tip:** This recipe contains uncooked egg. Make sure to use fresh, clean Grade A eggs. Keep chilled. Pregnant women, young children or the elderly are not advised to eat anything containing raw egg.

# Puffed Wheat Squares

*A can't-miss hit with kids, and they can help you make them too.*

| | | |
|---|---|---|
| **Puffed wheat cereal** | **6 cups** | **1.5 L** |
| **Brown sugar, packed** | **1/2 cup** | **125 mL** |
| **Corn syrup** | **1/3 cup** | **75 mL** |
| **Butter (or hard margarine)** | **1/4 cup** | **60 mL** |
| **Cocoa, sifted if lumpy** | **1 1/2 tbsp.** | **25 mL** |

Measure puffed wheat into large bowl.

Combine remaining 4 ingredients in small saucepan. Bring to a boil on medium. Heat and stir for 1 1/2 minutes. Remove from heat. Pour over cereal. Stir until coated. Press firmly into greased 8 x 8 inch (20 x 20 cm) pan. Let stand in pan on wire rack until cool. Cuts into 25 squares.

***1 square:** 57 Calories; 1.9 g Total Fat (0.5 g Mono, 0.1 g Poly, 1.2 g Sat); 5 mg Cholesterol; 10 g Carbohydrate; trace Fibre; 1 g Protein; 17 mg Sodium*

Pictured on page 35.

# Chocolate Confetti

*Much can be said about this square—simple to make, children and adults love it, and it freezes well. Plus it adds colour to a tray of goodies!*

| | | |
|---|---|---|
| **Semi-sweet chocolate chips** | **1 cup** | **250 mL** |
| **Smooth peanut butter** | **1/2 cup** | **125 mL** |
| **Butter (or hard margarine)** | **1/4 cup** | **60 mL** |
| **Bag of miniature multi-coloured marshmallows** | **9 oz.** | **250 g** |

Heat first 3 ingredients in large heavy saucepan on lowest heat, stirring often, until almost melted. Remove from heat. Stir until smooth. Let stand for about 15 minutes, until lukewarm.

Add marshmallows. Stir until coated. Press firmly into foil-lined 9 x 9 inch (22 x 22 cm) pan. Chill until firm. Cuts into 36 squares.

***1 square:** 77 Calories; 4.6 g Total Fat (0.8 g Mono, 0.1 g Poly, 2.0 g Sat); 3 mg Cholesterol; 9 g Carbohydrate; 1 g Fibre; 1 g Protein; 32 mg Sodium*

Pictured on page 35.

**Variation:** Add 1/2 cup (125 mL) chopped walnuts, or 1/2 cup (125 mL) medium unsweetened coconut.

# Fudgy Macaroons

*Crunchy butterscotch treats with a taste similar to brown sugar fudge.*

| | | |
|---|---|---|
| **Granulated sugar** | **1 1/2 cups** | **375 mL** |
| **Evaporated milk (or half-and-half cream)** | **1 cup** | **250 mL** |
| **Butter (or hard margarine)** | **1/4 cup** | **60 mL** |
| **Butterscotch chips** | **2 cups** | **500 mL** |
| **Vanilla extract** | **1 tsp.** | **5 mL** |
| **Cornflakes cereal** | **4 cups** | **1 L** |
| **Medium unsweetened coconut** | **2 1/2 cups** | **625 mL** |
| **Chopped walnuts** | **1 cup** | **250 mL** |

Combine first 3 ingredients in large saucepan. Heat on medium, stirring often, until mixture comes to a rolling boil. Remove from heat.

Add butterscotch chips and vanilla. Stir until chips are melted.

Add remaining 3 ingredients. Stir well. Spread evenly in greased 9 x 9 inch (22 x 22 cm) pan. Chill until set. Cuts into 36 squares.

***1 square:*** *191 Calories; 10.8 g Total Fat (0.9 g Mono, 1.7 g Poly, 7.8 g Sat); 6 mg Cholesterol; 22 g Carbohydrate; 1 g Fibre; 2 g Protein; 49 mg Sodium*

Pictured on page 18.

# Chow Mein Noodles

*You've probably had this as a drop cookie, but it's actually much easier to prepare in a pan. Handy to have in the freezer for kids' lunches.*

| | | |
|---|---|---|
| **Dry chow mein noodles, broken up** | **1 1/2 cups** | **375 mL** |
| **Chopped walnuts** | **1 cup** | **250 mL** |
| **Flaked coconut** | **1 cup** | **250 mL** |
| **Butterscotch chips** | **1 cup** | **250 mL** |
| **Semi-sweet chocolate chips** | **1 cup** | **250 mL** |

Combine first 3 ingredients in large bowl.

Heat butterscotch and chocolate chips in small, heavy saucepan on lowest heat, stirring often, until almost melted. Remove from heat. Stir until smooth. Pour over noodle mixture. Stir until coated. Spread evenly in foil-lined 8 x 8 inch (20 x 20 cm) pan. Chill until set. Cuts into 25 squares.

***1 square:*** *143 Calories; 9.5 g Total Fat (1.4 g Mono, 2.8 g Poly, 5.0 g Sat); 0 mg Cholesterol; 14 g Carbohydrate; 1 g Fibre; 2 g Protein; 27 mg Sodium*

Pictured on page 36.

# Tropical Treat

*Coffee flavours this square that is indeed a treat from the tropics.*

| | | |
|---|---|---|
| **Finely crushed vanilla wafers (about two 11 oz., 312 g boxes)** | **5 1/2 cups** | **1.4 L** |
| **Granulated sugar** | **1 cup** | **250 mL** |
| **Butter (or hard margarine)** | **3/4 cup** | **175 mL** |
| **Milk** | **3/4 cup** | **175 mL** |
| **Instant coffee granules** | **3 1/2 tsp.** | **17 mL** |
| **Dark (navy) rum (or 1/4 tsp., 1 mL, rum extract plus 4 tsp., 20 mL, water)** | **4 tsp.** | **20 mL** |
| **ICING** | | |
| **Icing (confectioner's) sugar** | **1 1/4 cups** | **300 mL** |
| **Butter (or hard margarine), softened** | **2 tbsp.** | **30 mL** |
| **Hot strong prepared coffee** | **4 tsp.** | **20 mL** |

Measure wafer crumbs into large bowl. Set aside.

Combine next 4 ingredients in small saucepan. Heat and stir on medium until butter is melted and mixture is boiling. Remove from heat.

Add rum. Stir. Pour over crumbs in bowl. Mix well, adding a few more crumbs if too soft (see Note). Spread evenly in greased 8 x 8 inch (20 x 20 cm) pan. Chill until firm.

**Icing:** Beat all 3 ingredients in medium bowl until smooth, adding more coffee or icing sugar as necessary until spreading consistency. Spread evenly over bottom layer. Let stand until set. Cuts into 25 squares.

*__1 square:__ 314 Calories; 12.5 g Total Fat (1.7 g Mono, 0.2 g Poly, 5.6 g Sat); 25 mg Cholesterol; 48 g Carbohydrate; 0 g Fibre; 3 g Protein; 247 mg Sodium*

Pictured on page 36.

**Note:** This does not firm up very much when chilled.

## *Paré Pointer*

*A friend has gone to a lot of work to serve you a deliciously rich lunch. It simply doesn't count, no matter what kind of a diet you are on—it's good manners, not a meal.*

# Cherry Wonder

*Aptly named, since many cannot decide what provides the underlying flavour. These should be kept chilled.*

| | | |
|---|---|---|
| Whole graham crackers | 12 – 13 | 12 – 13 |
| Egg yolk (large), see Safety Tip | 1 | 1 |
| Butter (or hard margarine), softened | 1/2 cup | 125 mL |
| Icing (confectioner's) sugar | 1 cup | 250 mL |
| Medium unsweetened coconut | 1 cup | 250 mL |
| Chopped maraschino cherries, well drained | 1/2 cup | 125 mL |
| Chopped walnuts | 1/2 cup | 125 mL |
| Mashed banana (about 1 medium) | 1/2 cup | 125 mL |
| WALNUT TOPPING | | |
| Butter (or hard margarine), softened | 3 tbsp. | 50 mL |
| Icing (confectioner's) sugar | 2 cups | 500 mL |
| Vanilla extract | 1/2 tsp. | 2 mL |
| Milk | 4 tsp. | 20 mL |
| Finely chopped walnuts | 1 – 2 tbsp. | 15 – 30 mL |

Line bottom of ungreased 9 x 9 inch (22 x 22 cm) pan with graham crackers, cutting to fit.

Beat next 3 ingredients in large bowl until combined.

Add next 4 ingredients. Stir well. Spread evenly over crackers in pan. Chill for at least 6 hours or overnight.

**Walnut Topping:** Beat first 4 ingredients in medium bowl until smooth, adding more milk or icing sugar as necessary until spreading consistency. Spread evenly over cherry nut layer.

Sprinkle with walnuts. Cuts into 36 squares.

***1 square:** 111 Calories; 6.3 g Total Fat (1.3 g Mono, 1.1 g Poly, 3.6 g Sat); 15 mg Cholesterol; 14 g Carbohydrate; 1 g Fibre; 1 g Protein; 33 mg Sodium*

Pictured on page 36.

**Safety Tip:** This recipe contains uncooked egg. Make sure to use fresh, clean Grade A eggs. Keep chilled. Pregnant women, young children or the elderly are not advised to eat anything containing raw egg.

# Chocolate Peanut Squares

*An abundance of chocolate melts with smooth peanut butter to fill your kitchen with a heavenly aroma.*

| | | |
|---|---|---|
| **Semi-sweet chocolate chips** | **1 1/2 cups** | **375 mL** |
| **Smooth peanut butter** | **3/4 cup** | **175 mL** |
| **Bran flakes cereal** | **3 cups** | **750 mL** |
| **Chopped pitted dates** | **1 1/3 cups** | **325 mL** |
| **Medium unsweetened coconut** | **2 tbsp.** | **30 mL** |

Heat chocolate chips and peanut butter in small, heavy saucepan on lowest heat, stirring often, until chocolate is almost melted. Remove from heat. Stir until smooth.

Add cereal and dates. Stir until coated. Press firmly into foil-lined 9 x 9 inch (22 x 22 cm) pan.

Sprinkle with coconut. Chill for at least 6 hours or overnight. Cuts into 36 squares.

***1 square:*** *95 Calories; 5.2 g Total Fat (0.7 g Mono, trace Poly, 2.0 g Sat); 0 mg Cholesterol; 13 g Carbohydrate; 2 g Fibre; 2 g Protein; 50 mg Sodium*

Pictured on page 36.

# Butterscotch Confetti

*This freezes so well that there is no excuse not to have it on hand. That is, if you keep it hidden.*

| | | |
|---|---|---|
| **Butterscotch chips** | **1 cup** | **250 mL** |
| **Smooth peanut butter** | **1/2 cup** | **125 mL** |
| **Butter (or hard margarine)** | **1/4 cup** | **60 mL** |
| **Bag of miniature multi-coloured marshmallows** | **9 oz.** | **250 g** |

Heat first 3 ingredients in large, heavy saucepan on lowest heat, stirring often, until chips are almost melted. Remove from heat. Stir until smooth. Let stand for about 15 minutes, until cooled to lukewarm.

*(continued on next page)*

Add marshmallows. Stir until coated. Press firmly into foil-lined 9 x 9 inch (22 x 22 cm) pan. Chill until firm. Cuts into 36 squares.

*1 square: 90 Calories; 4.9 g Total Fat (0.3 g Mono, 0.1 g Poly, 3.0 g Sat); 3.3 mg Cholesterol; 11 g Carbohydrate; trace Fibre; 1 g Protein; 36 mg Sodium*

Pictured on page 36.

**Variation:** Add 1/2 cup (125 mL) chopped walnuts, or 1/2 cup (125 mL) medium unsweetened coconut.

# Chocolate Carousels

*This has a peanut butter flavour and a nice fruity look. Looks wonderful, even without the glaze.*

| | | |
|---|---|---|
| **Icing (confectioner's) sugar** | **2 cups** | **500 mL** |
| **Smooth peanut butter** | **2 cups** | **500 mL** |
| **Butter (or hard margarine), softened** | **2 tbsp.** | **30 mL** |
| **Salt** | **1/8 tsp.** | **0.5 mL** |
| **Chopped maraschino cherries, well drained** | **1 cup** | **250 mL** |
| **Chopped pecans (or walnuts)** | **1 cup** | **250 mL** |
| **Chopped pitted dates** | **1 cup** | **250 mL** |
| **TOPPING** | | |
| **Semi-sweet chocolate baking squares, (1 oz., 28 g, each), chopped (see Note)** | **4** | **4** |
| **Smooth peanut butter** | **2 tbsp.** | **30 mL** |

Combine first 4 ingredients in large bowl.

Add next 3 ingredients. Mix well. Press firmly into foil-lined 8 x 8 inch (20 x 20 cm) pan.

**Topping:** Heat chocolate and peanut butter in small, heavy saucepan on lowest heat, stirring often, until chocolate is almost melted. Remove from heat. Stir until smooth. Spread evenly over bottom layer. Chill until firm. Cuts into 25 squares.

*1 square: 255 Calories; 16.4 g Total Fat (2.4 g Mono, 1.1 g Poly, 3.5 g Sat); 2.4 mg Cholesterol; 26 g Carbohydrate; 3 g Fibre; 6 g Protein; 121 mg Sodium*

Pictured on page 36.

**Note:** You can use 2/3 cup (150 mL) semi-sweet chocolate chips in place of the chocolate baking squares.

# Chocolate Cherry Creams

*Eats more like a candy than a roll—creamy and mouth-watering.*

| | | |
|---|---|---|
| **Semi-sweet chocolate chips** | **1 cup** | **250 mL** |
| **Evaporated milk (or half-and-half cream)** | **1/2 cup** | **125 mL** |
| **Icing (confectioner's) sugar** | **3 cups** | **750 mL** |
| **Chopped walnuts** | **1/2 cup** | **125 mL** |
| **Chopped maraschino cherries, well drained** | **1/3 cup** | **75 mL** |
| **Medium unsweetened coconut** | **1/2 cup** | **125 mL** |

Heat chocolate chips and evaporated milk in small, heavy saucepan on lowest heat, stirring often, until chocolate is almost melted. Remove from heat. Stir until smooth.

Add next 3 ingredients. Chill for about 1 hour until firm. Divide mixture in half. Roll each half into 6 inch (15 cm) long log, about 1 1/2 inches (3.8 cm) in diameter.

Sprinkle coconut evenly over sheet of waxed paper, slightly longer than logs. Roll each log in coconut until coated. Wrap with plastic wrap. Chill for about 2 hours until firm. Cut into thin slices. Makes about 48 slices.

Pictured on page 36.

***1 slice:*** *64 Calories; 2.4 g Total Fat (0.5 g Mono, 0.6 g Poly, 1.2 g Sat); 1 mg Cholesterol; 11 g Carbohydrate; trace Fibre; 1 g Protein; 3 mg Sodium*

1. Puffed Wheat Squares, page 28
2. Rainbow Pastel, page 23
3. Chocolate Confetti, page 28
4. Bridge Peel Dainties, page 26
5. Butterscotch Coconut Squares, page 25
6. Snow Log, page 26
7. Jellied Marshmallows, page 16
8. Chocolate Coconut Layer, page 19

Props courtesy of: Chintz & Company

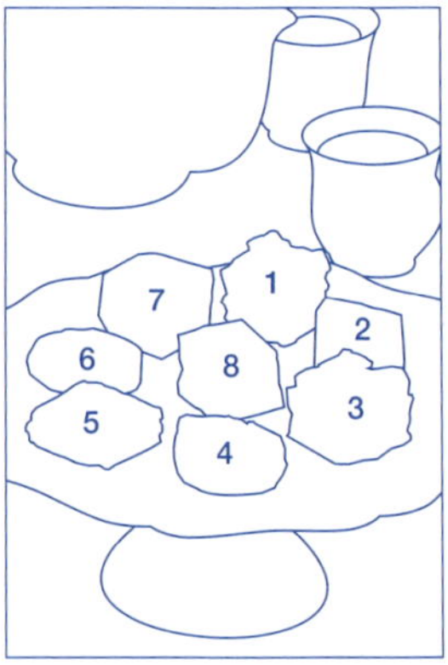

# Nummies

*A not-too-sweet bar. The taste will win you over, and you'll be saying "nummy!" after the first bite.*

| | | |
|---|---|---|
| **Whole graham crackers (about 32), broken up** | **8 oz.** | **225 g** |
| **Miniature marshmallows** | **2 1/2 cups** | **625 mL** |
| **Butter (or hard margarine)** | **1/2 cup** | **125 mL** |
| **Granulated sugar** | **1/2 cup** | **125 mL** |
| **Large egg, fork-beaten (see Safety Tip)** | **1** | **1** |
| **GLAZE** | | |
| **Icing (confectioner's) sugar** | **1 cup** | **250 mL** |
| **Milk** | **1 tbsp.** | **15 mL** |
| **Vanilla extract** | **1/2 tsp.** | **2 mL** |

Combine graham cracker pieces and marshmallows in large bowl.

Combine next 3 ingredients in small, heavy saucepan. Heat on low, stirring often, until mixture is syrupy. Pour over marshmallow mixture. Stir until coated. Press firmly into greased 8 x 8 inch (20 x 20 cm) pan.

**Glaze:** Beat all 3 ingredients in small bowl until smooth, adding more milk or icing sugar as necessary until barely pourable consistency. Drizzle over bottom layer. Let stand until set. Cuts into 25 squares.

*__1 square:__ 106 Calories; 4.4 g Total Fat (1.2 g Mono, 0.3 g Poly, 2.5 g Sat); 18 mg Cholesterol; 16 g Carbohydrate; trace Fibre; 1 g Protein; 58 mg Sodium*

Pictured at left.

**Safety Tip:** This recipe contains uncooked egg. Make sure to use fresh, clean Grade A eggs. Keep chilled. Pregnant women, young children or the elderly are not advised to eat anything containing raw egg.

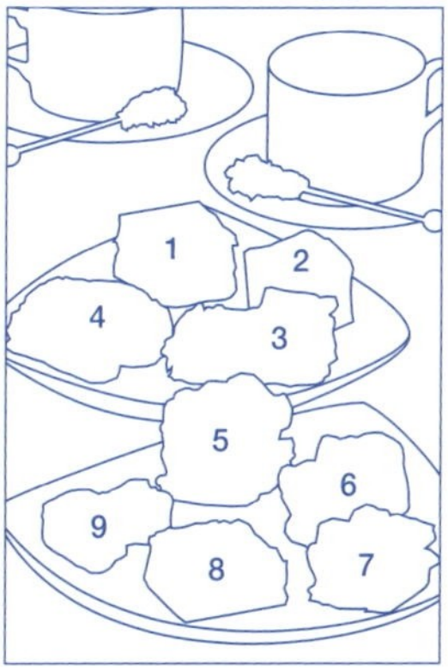


1. Chocolate Carousels, page 33
2. Tropical Treat, page 30
3. Chow Mein Noodles, page 29
4. TV Roll, page 27
5. Nummies, above
6. Chocolate Peanut Squares, page 32
7. Butterscotch Confetti, page 32
8. Cherry Wonder, page 31
9. Chocolate Cherry Creams, page 34

# Marshmallow Roll

*This is such a neat-looking sweet on any plate.*

| | | |
|---|---|---|
| Unsweetened chocolate baking squares (1 oz., 28 g, each), chopped | 2 | 2 |
| Graham cracker crumbs | 2 cups | 450 mL |
| Can of sweetened condensed milk | 11 oz. | 300 mL |
| Finely chopped walnuts | 1/2 cup | 125 mL |
| Large marshmallows | 20 | 20 |
| Medium unsweetened coconut | 1/2 cup | 125 mL |

Heat chocolate in large heavy saucepan on lowest heat, stirring often, until almost melted. Remove from heat. Stir until smooth.

Add next 3 ingredients. Stir well. Divide mixture in half. Press one half between 2 sheets of parchment paper. Roll out to 4 1/2 x 12 inch (11 x 30 cm) rectangle. Remove top sheet of parchment paper. Set aside.

Place 10 marshmallows, end-to-end, along centre of chocolate mixture. Bring sides up over marshmallows. Pinch to seal.

Sprinkle 1/4 cup (60 mL) coconut evenly over reserved parchment paper, slightly longer than log. Roll log in coconut until coated. Wrap with plastic wrap. Repeat with other portion, marshmallows and coconut. Chill until firm. Cut into 1/2 inch (6 mm) slices. Makes about 48 slices.

*__1 slice:__ 62 Calories; 2.3 g Total Fat (0.3 g Mono, 0.7 g Poly, 0.9 g Sat); 2 mg Cholesterol; 10 g Carbohydrate; trace Fibre; 1 g Protein; 32 mg Sodium*

Pictured on page 53.

# Krispy Krunch Bars

*Little kids like these as much as big kids!*

| | | |
|---|---|---|
| Crisp rice cereal | 2 1/2 cups | 625 mL |
| Icing (confectioner's) sugar | 2 1/2 cups | 625 mL |
| Smooth peanut butter | 2 cups | 500 mL |
| Butter (or hard margarine), melted | 1/4 cup | 60 mL |
| Chopped walnuts (optional) | 1/2 cup | 125 mL |
| Semi-sweet chocolate chips | 2/3 cup | 150 mL |
| Butter (or hard margarine) | 1 tbsp. | 15 mL |

*(continued on next page)*

Combine first 5 ingredients in large bowl. Press firmly into foil-lined 9 x 9 inch (22 x 22 cm) pan.

Heat chocolate chips and butter in small, heavy saucepan on lowest heat, stirring often, until almost melted. Remove from heat. Stir until smooth. Spread evenly over bottom layer. Let stand until set. Cuts into 36 squares.

*1 square: 153 Calories; 10.1 g Total Fat (0.7 g Mono, 0.1 g Poly, 3.1 g Sat); 4 mg Cholesterol; 15 g Carbohydrate; 1 g Fibre; 3 g Protein; 96 mg Sodium*

Pictured on page 53.

# Pineapple Log

*A pretty little roll to have on hand—it keeps well in the freezer.*

| | | |
|---|---|---|
| **Cream cheese, softened** | **4 oz.** | **125 g** |
| **Finely crushed vanilla wafers (about 96), see Note 1** | **3 cups** | **750 mL** |
| **Can of crushed pineapple, well drained** | **14 oz.** | **398 mL** |
| **Icing (confectioner's) sugar** | **1 cup** | **250 mL** |
| **Salt** | **1/4 tsp.** | **1 mL** |
| **Miniature multi-coloured marshmallows, cut into quarters (see Note 2)** | **1/2 cup** | **125 mL** |
| **Shredded coconut** | **1/2 cup** | **125 mL** |
| **Drops of yellow liquid food colouring** | **2 – 3** | **2 – 3** |

Beat cream cheese in large bowl until smooth. Add next 4 ingredients. Mix well.

Add marshmallows. Mix well. Divide into 2 portions. Roll each half into 6 inch (15 cm) long log, about 2 inches (5 cm) in diameter, working in more crumbs or icing sugar if needed to make firm.

Measure coconut into container with lid. Add food colouring. Shake to distribute food colouring evenly. Sprinkle coconut evenly over sheet of waxed paper, slightly longer than logs. Roll each log in coconut until coated. Wrap with plastic wrap. Chill for about 2 hours until firm. Cut into 1/4 inch (6 mm) slices. Makes about 48 slices.

*1 slice: 80 Calories; 2.7 g Total Fat (trace Mono, trace Poly, 1 g Sat); 4 mg Cholesterol; 13 g Carbohydrate; trace Fibre; 1 g Protein; 75 mg Sodium*

Pictured on page 53.

**Note 1:** This is equal to approximately one 11 ounce (312 gram) box of vanilla wafers.

**Note 2:** Using scissors makes for easy cutting of the marshmallows.

# Nanaimo Bars

*Looks so good you'll want to make this your special occasion bar. You can make it the day before or have it ready in the freezer.*

| | | |
|---|---|---|
| **BOTTOM LAYER** | | |
| **Butter (or hard margarine)** | **1/2 cup** | **125 mL** |
| **Cocoa, sifted if lumpy** | **1/3 cup** | **75 mL** |
| **Granulated sugar** | **1/4 cup** | **60 mL** |
| **Large egg, fork-beaten** | **1** | **1** |
| **Graham cracker crumbs** | **1 3/4 cups** | **425 mL** |
| **Medium unsweetened coconut** | **3/4 cup** | **175 mL** |
| **Finely chopped walnuts** | **1/2 cup** | **125 mL** |
| **MIDDLE LAYER** | | |
| **Icing (confectioner's) sugar** | **2 cups** | **500 mL** |
| **Butter (or hard margarine), softened** | **1/2 cup** | **125 mL** |
| **Milk** | **3 tbsp.** | **50 mL** |
| **Vanilla custard powder** | **2 tbsp.** | **30 mL** |
| **TOP LAYER** | | |
| **Semi-sweet chocolate chips** | **2/3 cup** | **150 mL** |
| **Butter (or hard margarine)** | **2 tbsp.** | **30 mL** |

**Bottom Layer:** Heat and stir first 3 ingredients in medium, heavy saucepan on medium-low until smooth. Add egg. Stir until thickened. Remove from heat.

Add next 3 ingredients. Stir well. Press firmly into ungreased 9 x 9 inch (22 x 22 cm) pan.

**Middle Layer:** Beat all 4 ingredients in medium bowl until smooth. Spread evenly over bottom layer.

**Top Layer:** Heat chocolate chips and butter in small, heavy saucepan on lowest heat, stirring often, until chocolate is almost melted. Remove from heat. Stir until smooth. Cool to lukewarm. Spread evenly over middle layer. Chill until top layer is set. Cuts into 36 squares.

***1 square:** 143 Calories; 9.3 g Total Fat (2.2 g Mono, 1.2 g Poly, 5.3 g Sat); 21 mg Cholesterol; 15 g Carbohydrate; 1 g Fibre; 1 g Protein; 75 mg Sodium*

Pictured on page 53.

# Peanut Krispy Squares

*The chocolate frosting on this cereal square makes it taste and look amazing.*

| | | |
|---|---|---|
| Crisp rice cereal | 2 cups | 500 mL |
| Unsalted peanuts | 1 cup | 250 mL |
| Brown sugar, packed | 1/2 cup | 125 mL |
| Corn syrup | 1/2 cup | 125 mL |
| Smooth peanut butter | 1/2 cup | 125 mL |
| Butter (or hard margarine) | 4 tsp. | 20 mL |
| ICING | | |
| Icing (confectioner's) sugar | 1/2 cup | 125 mL |
| Butter (or hard margarine) | 1/4 cup | 60 mL |
| Milk | 3 tbsp. | 50 mL |
| Vanilla extract | 1/2 tsp. | 2 mL |
| Icing (confectioner's) sugar | 1 1/2 cups | 375 mL |
| Cocoa, sifted if lumpy | 2 tbsp. | 30 mL |

Combine cereal and peanuts in large bowl.

Combine next 4 ingredients in small, heavy saucepan. Heat and stir on low until melted and smooth. Pour over cereal mixture. Stir until coated. Press firmly into greased 8 x 8 inch (20 x 20 cm) pan.

**Icing:** Heat and stir first 4 ingredients in small saucepan on medium until melted. Bring to a boil. Reduce heat to medium-low. Simmer, uncovered, for 2 minutes, stirring occasionally. Transfer to medium bowl. Cool for about 30 minutes until lukewarm.

Add icing sugar and cocoa. Beat until light and creamy, adding more milk or icing sugar as necessary until spreading consistency. Spread evenly over cereal layer. Let stand until icing is set. Cuts into 25 squares.

***1 square:*** *169 Calories; 8.2 g Total Fat (2.1 g Mono, 1.0 g Poly, 2.5 g Sat); 6.5 mg Cholesterol; 23 g Carbohydrate; 1 g Fibre; 3 g Protein; 68 mg Sodium*

Pictured on page 53.

## *Paré Pointer*

*Keep talking while eating—the stomach doesn't know what is going on when the throat is so busy doing its own thing.*

# Chocolate Coffee Squares

*You'll find this stovetop square both fast to make and scrumptious to eat.*

| | | |
|---|---|---|
| Whole graham crackers | 12 – 13 | 12 – 13 |
| Butter (or hard margarine) | 3/4 cup | 175 mL |
| Brown sugar, packed | 2/3 cup | 150 mL |
| Milk | 1/2 cup | 125 mL |
| Semi-sweet chocolate chips | 1/3 cup | 75 mL |
| Graham cracker crumbs | 1 1/4 cups | 300 mL |
| Chopped walnuts | 1 cup | 250 mL |
| Whole graham crackers | 12 – 13 | 12 – 13 |
| COFFEE ICING | | |
| Icing (confectioner's) sugar | 1 1/4 cups | 300 mL |
| Cocoa, sifted if lumpy | 1/4 cup | 60 mL |
| Butter (or hard margarine), softened | 3 tbsp. | 50 mL |
| Hot strong prepared coffee | 1 1/2 tbsp. | 25 mL |

Line ungreased 9 x 9 inch (22 x 22 cm) pan with first amount of graham crackers, cutting to fit. Set aside.

Combine next 3 ingredients in large saucepan. Bring to a boil on medium, stirring occasionally. Remove from heat.

Add chocolate chips. Stir until melted. Add graham crumbs and walnuts. Stir well. Spread evenly over crackers in pan.

Cover with second amount of graham crackers, cutting to fit. Cool.

**Coffee Icing:** Beat all 4 ingredients in medium bowl, adding more coffee or icing sugar as necessary until spreading consistency. Spread evenly over graham crackers. Let stand, covered, for at least 6 hours or overnight until crackers are softened. Cuts into 36 squares.

***1 square:*** *130 Calories; 8.1 g Total Fat (1.9 g Mono, 1.9 g Poly, 3.6 g Sat); 13 mg Cholesterol; 14 g Carbohydrate; 1 g Fibre; 1 g Protein; 68 mg Sodium*

Pictured on page 53.

# Festive Fruit Squares

*Make this two or three days before you need to cut it to allow the flavours to mellow.*

| | | |
|---|---|---|
| Chopped mixed glazed fruit | 1 cup | 250 mL |
| Chopped walnuts | 1 cup | 250 mL |
| Chopped pitted dates | 3/4 cup | 175 mL |
| Raisins (or currants) | 3/4 cup | 175 mL |
| Chopped red glazed cherries | 1/4 cup | 60 mL |
| Miniature marshmallows | 2 cups | 500 mL |
| Evaporated milk (or half-and-half cream) | 2/3 cup | 150 mL |
| Frozen concentrated orange juice, thawed | 6 tbsp. | 100 mL |
| Graham cracker crumbs | 4 cups | 1 L |
| Ground cinnamon | 1 tsp. | 5 mL |
| Ground nutmeg | 1 tsp. | 5 mL |
| Ground cloves | 1/2 tsp. | 2 mL |
| ICING | | |
| Icing (confectioner's) sugar | 1 1/2 cups | 375 mL |
| Butter (or hard margarine), softened | 3 tbsp. | 50 mL |
| Milk | 1 1/2 tbsp. | 25 mL |
| Vanilla extract | 1/2 tsp. | 2 mL |

Combine first 5 ingredients in large bowl.

Combine next 3 ingredients in medium saucepan. Heat and stir on medium until marshmallows are melted. Remove from heat. Pour over fruit mixture.

Add next 4 ingredients. Mix well. Press firmly into foil-lined 9 x 9 inch (22 x 22 cm) pan. Cover tightly. Chill for at least 2 days.

**Icing:** Beat all 4 ingredients in small bowl until smooth, adding more milk or icing sugar as necessary until spreading consistency. Spread evenly over bottom layer. Cuts into 36 squares.

***1 square:*** *150 Calories; 4.4 g Total Fat (1.0 g Mono, 2.0 g Poly, 1.2 g Sat); 4 mg Cholesterol; 27 g Carbohydrate; 1 g Fibre; 2 g Protein; 76 mg Sodium*

Pictured on page 53.

# Cherry Nut Bars

*Sometimes called an Oh Henry Bar, this square is a chock-full layer of nuts and cherries smothered by rich pink icing.*

| | | |
|---|---|---|
| **Whole graham crackers** | **12 – 13** | **12 – 13** |
| **Brown sugar, packed** | **1 cup** | **250 mL** |
| **Butter (or hard margarine)** | **1/2 cup** | **125 mL** |
| **Milk** | **1/2 cup** | **125 mL** |
| **Graham cracker crumbs** | **1 1/3 cups** | **325 mL** |
| **Chopped walnuts** | **1 cup** | **250 mL** |
| **Medium unsweetened coconut** | **1 cup** | **250 mL** |
| **Chopped maraschino cherries, well drained** | **1/4 cup** | **60 mL** |
| **ICING** | | |
| **Icing (confectioner's) sugar** | **1 1/2 cups** | **375 mL** |
| **Butter (or hard margarine), softened** | **3 tbsp.** | **50 mL** |
| **Milk** | **1 1/2 tbsp.** | **25 mL** |
| **Vanilla extract** | **1/2 tsp.** | **2 mL** |
| **Drop of red liquid food colouring** | **1** | **1** |

Line ungreased 9 x 9 inch (22 x 22 cm) pan with graham crackers, cutting to fit. Set aside.

Combine next 3 ingredients in small, heavy saucepan. Bring to a boil on medium, stirring occasionally. Reduce heat to medium-low. Simmer for 2 minutes. Remove from heat.

Add next 4 ingredients. Stir well. Spread evenly over crackers in pan. Cool.

**Icing:** Beat all 5 ingredients in medium bowl until smooth, adding more milk or icing sugar as necessary until spreading consistency. Spread evenly over bottom layer. Let stand, covered, for at least 6 hours or overnight until crackers are softened. Cuts into 36 squares.

*__1 square:__ 132 Calories; 7.5 g Total Fat (1.5 g Mono, 1.9 g Poly, 3.7 g Sat); 9 mg Cholesterol; 16 g Carbohydrate; 1 g Fibre; 1 g Protein; 56 mg Sodium*

Pictured on page 53.

# Millionaire Squares

*They're not expensive, but they're super rich!*

| | | |
|---|---|---|
| **CRUST** | | |
| **Butter (or hard margarine)** | **1/2 cup** | **125 mL** |
| **Finely crushed crisp oatmeal cookies** | **2 cups** | **500 mL** |
| **CHOCOLATE FILLING** | | |
| **Semi-sweet chocolate baking squares, (1 oz., 28 g, each), chopped** | **3** | **3** |
| **Butter (or hard margarine)** | **1/2 cup** | **125 mL** |
| **Large egg (see Safety Tip)** | **1** | **1** |
| **Icing (confectioner's) sugar** | **2 cups** | **500 mL** |
| **Chopped walnuts** | **1/2 cup** | **125 mL** |

**Crust:** Heat butter in small saucepan on medium until melted. Remove from heat. Add cookie crumbs. Stir well. Reserve 1/4 cup (60 mL) in small bowl. Press remaining crumb mixture firmly into ungreased 8 x 8 inch (20 x 20 cm) pan. Bake in 350°F (175°C) oven for 5 minutes. Let stand in pan on wire rack until cool.

**Chocolate Filling:** Heat chocolate and butter in small, heavy saucepan on lowest heat, stirring often, until chocolate is almost melted. Remove from heat. Stir until smooth. Add egg. Beat well. Add icing sugar. Beat until smooth. Stir in walnuts. Spread evenly over crust. Sprinkle with reserved crumb mixture. Chill until set. Cuts into 36 squares.

***1 square:*** *123 Calories; 8.1 g Total Fat (2.1 g Mono, 1.2 g Poly, 4.0 g Sat); 20 mg Cholesterol; 13 g Carbohydrate; trace Fibre; 1 g Protein; 67 mg Sodium*

Pictured on page 53.

**Safety Tip:** This recipe uses raw eggs. Make sure to use fresh, clean Grade A eggs. Keep chilled. Pregnant women, young children or the elderly are not advised to eat anything containing raw egg.

### *Paré Pointer*

*A good time to eat is when you are daydreaming. If you eat without thinking about it, it can't count against you.*

# Marshmallow Squares

*The flavour and texture of these are so delicious that they're always among the first to disappear at a gathering.*

| | | |
|---|---|---|
| **BOTTOM LAYER** | | |
| All-purpose flour | 1 1/2 cups | 375 mL |
| Butter (or hard margarine), softened | 3/4 cup | 175 mL |
| Brown sugar, packed | 1/3 cup | 75 mL |
| **TOP LAYER** | | |
| Envelope of unflavoured gelatin (about 1 tbsp., 15 mL) | 1/4 oz. | 7 g |
| Cold water | 3/4 cup | 175 mL |
| Granulated sugar | 3/4 cup | 175 mL |
| Salt | 1/8 tsp. | 0.5 mL |
| Icing (confectioner's) sugar | 3/4 cup | 175 mL |
| Almond extract | 1/2 tsp. | 2 mL |
| Vanilla extract | 1/2 tsp. | 2 mL |
| Red liquid food colouring | 1/2 tsp. | 2 mL |

**Bottom Layer:** Mix first 3 ingredients in small bowl until mixture resembles fine crumbs. Press firmly into ungreased 9 x 9 inch (22 x 22 cm) pan. Bake in 325°F (160°C) oven for about 25 minutes until golden. Let stand in pan on wire rack until cool.

**Top Layer:** Sprinkle gelatin over cold water in small saucepan. Let stand for 1 minute. Add sugar and salt. Heat and stir on low until sugar is dissolved. Remove from heat.

Whisk in icing sugar. Transfer to large bowl. Chill, uncovered, for about 20 minutes, stirring every 5 minutes, until very thick. Beat until foamy.

Add remaining 3 ingredients. Beat on high for about 10 minutes, until thick and soft peaks form. Spread evenly over bottom layer. Chill for at least 6 hours or overnight. Cuts into 36 squares.

***1 square:*** *85 Calories; 3.8 g Total Fat (1.0 g Mono, 0.1 g Poly, 2.4 g Sat); 10 mg Cholesterol; 12 g Carbohydrate; trace Fibre; 1 g Protein; 36 mg Sodium*

Pictured on divider page.

# Hermit Slice

*An old-fashioned favourite. Not too rich or too sweet.*

| | | |
|---|---|---|
| Large egg | 1 | 1 |
| Butter (or hard margarine), softened | 1/4 cup | 60 mL |
| Fancy (mild) molasses | 1/4 cup | 60 mL |
| Granulated sugar | 1/4 cup | 60 mL |
| Raisins (or currants) | 1/2 cup | 125 mL |
| Chopped walnuts | 1/4 cup | 60 mL |
| All-purpose flour | 3/4 cup | 175 mL |
| Baking powder | 1 tsp. | 5 mL |
| Ground cinnamon | 1/2 tsp. | 2 mL |
| Ground cloves | 1/4 tsp. | 1 mL |
| Salt | 1/4 tsp. | 1 mL |
| Baking soda | 1/8 tsp. | 0.5 mL |
| Ground allspice | 1/8 tsp. | 0.5 mL |
| Ground mace | 1/8 tsp. | 0.5 mL |
| Ground nutmeg | 1/8 tsp. | 0.5 mL |
| ICING | | |
| Brown sugar, packed | 1/3 cup | 75 mL |
| Butter (or hard margarine) | 3 tbsp. | 50 mL |
| Milk | 2 tbsp. | 30 mL |
| Icing (confectioner's) sugar | 1 cup | 250 mL |

Beat first 4 ingredients in large bowl until combined. Add raisins and walnuts. Mix well.

Combine next 9 ingredients in small bowl. Add to raisin mixture. Stir well. Spread evenly in greased 8 x 8 inch (20 x 20 cm) pan. Bake in 350°F (175°C) oven for about 20 minutes, until set. Let stand in pan on wire rack until cool.

**Icing:** Combine first 3 ingredients in small saucepan. Heat and stir on medium until melted. Bring to a boil. Reduce heat to medium-low. Simmer, uncovered, for 2 minutes, stirring occasionally. Transfer to medium bowl. Cool for about 30 minutes until lukewarm.

Add icing sugar. Beat until light and creamy, adding more milk or icing sugar as necessary until spreading consistency. Spread evenly over bottom layer. Cuts into 25 squares.

***1 square:*** *110 Calories; 4.2 g Total Fat (1.0 g Mono, 0.7 g Poly, 2.2 g Sat); 17 mg Cholesterol; 18 g Carbohydrate; trace Fibre; 1 g Protein; 81 mg Sodium*

Pictured on page 53.

# Lemon Slice

*A flashy square with a light-textured chiffon topping.*

| | | |
|---|---|---|
| **BOTTOM LAYER** | | |
| **Butter (or hard margarine)** | **1/2 cup** | **125 mL** |
| **Graham cracker crumbs** | **2 cups** | **500 mL** |
| **Granulated sugar** | **1/4 cup** | **60 mL** |
| **TOP LAYER** | | |
| **Egg yolks (large)** | **3** | **3** |
| **Granulated sugar** | **3/4 cup** | **175 mL** |
| **All-purpose flour** | **1/3 cup** | **75 mL** |
| **Lemon juice** | **1/4 cup** | **60 mL** |
| **Water** | **1 tbsp.** | **15 mL** |
| **Grated lemon zest (see Tip, page 60)** | **2 tsp.** | **10 mL** |
| **Egg whites (large), room temperature** | **3** | **3** |

**Bottom Layer:** Melt butter in medium saucepan on medium. Remove from heat. Add graham crumbs and sugar. Stir until well mixed. Reserve 1/4 cup (60 mL) for topping. Press remaining crumb mixture firmly into ungreased 9 x 9 inch (22 x 22 cm) pan. Bake in 350°F (175°C) oven for 10 minutes. Cool slightly.

**Top Layer:** Combine first 6 ingredients in small, heavy saucepan. Heat and stir on medium until thickened. Remove from heat.

Beat egg whites in small bowl until stiff peaks form. Fold into hot lemon mixture. Spread evenly over bottom layer. Sprinkle with reserved crumb mixture. Bake for 3 to 5 minutes, until set. Let stand on wire rack until cool. Cuts into 36 squares.

***1 square:*** *74 Calories; 3.4 g Total Fat (1.0 g Mono, 0.3 g Poly, 1.8 g Sat); 24 mg Cholesterol; 10 g Carbohydrate; trace Fibre; 1 g Protein; 51 mg Sodium*

Pictured on page 53.

### *Paré Pointer*

*Eating children's leftover food doesn't count—that is being thrifty.*

# Ginger Shortbread

*Candied ginger adds a distinct and pleasant flavour to traditional shortbread.*

| | | |
|---|---|---|
| **All-purpose flour** | **2 cups** | **500 mL** |
| **Butter, softened** | **1 cup** | **250 mL** |
| **Icing (confectioner's) sugar** | **1/2 cup** | **125 mL** |
| **Ground ginger** | **1 tsp.** | **5 mL** |
| **Minced crystallized ginger** | **1/3 cup** | **75 mL** |

Mix first 4 ingredients in medium bowl until crumbly.

Add ginger. Stir well. Press firmly into ungreased 9 x 9 inch (22 x 22 cm) pan. Prick entire surface of dough with fork through to bottom of pan. Bake in 300°F (150°C) oven for about 55 minutes until starting to turn golden. Cool slightly. Cut while still warm into 36 squares.

***1 square:** 81 Calories; 5.1 g Total Fat (1.3 g Mono, 0.2 g Poly, 3.2 g Sat); 13 mg Cholesterol; 8 g Carbohydrate; trace Fibre; 1 g Protein; 37 mg Sodium*

Pictured on page 54.

# Banana Oat Squares

*A rich-looking square with a light taste.*

| | | |
|---|---|---|
| **Butter (or hard margarine), softened** | **6 tbsp.** | **100 mL** |
| **Brown sugar, packed** | **1/2 cup** | **125 mL** |
| **Large egg** | **1** | **1** |
| **Mashed banana (about 1 1/2 medium)** | **3/4 cup** | **175 mL** |
| **Salt** | **1/4 tsp.** | **1 mL** |
| **Quick-cooking rolled oats** | **2 cups** | **500 mL** |
| **Chopped walnuts** | **1/3 cup** | **75 mL** |

Beat butter and brown sugar in medium bowl. Add egg. Beat well. Add banana and salt. Beat until combined.

Add rolled oats and walnuts. Stir until combined. Spread evenly in greased 8 x 8 inch (20 x 20 cm) pan. Bake in 350°F (175°C) oven for about 55 minutes until wooden pick inserted in centre comes out clean. Let stand in pan on wire rack until cool. Cuts into 25 squares.

***1 square:** 87 Calories; 4.5 g Total Fat (0.9 g Mono, 0.9 g Poly, 1.9 g Sat); 16 mg Cholesterol; 11 g Carbohydrate; 1 g Fibre; 2 g Protein; 47 mg Sodium*

Pictured on page 54.

# Matrimonial Squares

*A square that symbolizes marriage—a strong base with sweet filling. Perfect for bridal showers, weddings or anniversaries.*

| | | |
|---|---|---|
| **CRUST** | | |
| Quick-cooking rolled oats | 1 1/2 cups | 375 mL |
| All-purpose flour | 1 1/4 cups | 300 mL |
| Brown sugar, packed | 1 cup | 250 mL |
| Butter (or hard margarine), softened | 1 cup | 250 mL |
| Baking soda | 1 tsp. | 5 mL |
| Salt | 1/2 tsp. | 2 mL |
| **FILLING** | | |
| Chopped pitted dates | 1 1/2 cups | 375 mL |
| Water | 2/3 cup | 150 mL |
| Granulated sugar | 1/2 cup | 125 mL |

**Crust:** Mix all 6 ingredients in large bowl until crumbly. Press 2/3 of mixture firmly into greased 9 x 9 inch (22 x 22 cm) pan. Reserve remaining oat mixture.

**Filling:** Combine all 3 ingredients in medium saucepan. Bring to a boil on medium. Reduce heat to medium-low. Simmer, uncovered, for 5 to 10 minutes, until dates are softened and water is almost evaporated. Add more water while simmering if necessary to soften dates. Spread filling evenly over crust. Sprinkle reserved oat mixture evenly over top. Press down gently. Bake in 350°F (175°C) oven for about 30 minutes until golden brown. Let stand in pan on wire rack until cool. Cuts into 36 squares.

***1 square:*** *126 Calories; 5.3 g Total Fat (1.3 g Mono, 0.2 g Poly, 3.2 g Sat); 13 mg Cholesterol; 20 g Carbohydrate; 1 g Fibre; 1 g Protein; 105 mg Sodium*

Pictured on page 54.

### *Paré Pointer*

*Be sure to fill up your plate to overflowing. Then if you use proper manners, namely leave a bit of food, you will already have had your share.*

# Black Bottom Slice

*A sweet and nutty filling between two chocolate layers. So tempting!*

| | | |
|---|---|---|
| **BOTTOM LAYER** | | |
| All-purpose flour | 1 cup | 250 mL |
| Butter (or hard margarine), softened | 1/2 cup | 125 mL |
| Cocoa, sifted if lumpy | 1/4 cup | 60 mL |
| Granulated sugar | 1/4 cup | 60 mL |
| **SECOND LAYER** | | |
| Large eggs | 2 | 2 |
| Brown sugar, packed | 1 1/4 cups | 300 mL |
| Medium unsweetened coconut | 1 cup | 250 mL |
| Chopped walnuts | 3/4 cup | 175 mL |
| All-purpose flour | 1 tsp. | 5 mL |
| Baking powder | 1 tsp. | 5 mL |
| Vanilla extract | 1 tsp. | 5 mL |
| **ICING** | | |
| Icing (confectioner's) sugar | 1 1/4 cups | 300 mL |
| Cocoa, sifted if lumpy | 1/4 cup | 60 mL |
| Butter (or hard margarine), softened | 3 tbsp. | 50 mL |
| Hot strong prepared coffee | 1 1/2 tbsp. | 25 mL |

**Bottom Layer:** Mix all 4 ingredients in medium bowl until crumbly. Press firmly into ungreased 9 x 9 inch (22 x 22 cm) pan. Bake in 350°F (175°C) oven for 15 minutes.

**Second Layer:** Beat eggs until frothy. Add next 6 ingredients. Stir well. Spread evenly over bottom layer. Bake for 30 minutes. Let stand in pan on wire rack until cool.

**Icing:** Beat all 4 ingredients in small bowl until smooth, adding more coffee or icing sugar as necessary until spreading consistency. Spread evenly over second layer. Cuts into 36 squares.

***1 square:** 131 Calories; 6.8 g Total Fat (1.2 g Mono, 1.3 g Poly, 3.6 g Sat); 21 mg Cholesterol; 17 g Carbohydrate; 1 g Fibre; 1 g Protein; 47 mg Sodium*

Pictured on page 54.

# Nutty Bars

*These squares are the nuttiest you could wish for.*

| | | |
|---|---|---|
| **Large egg** | **1** | **1** |
| **Brown sugar, packed** | **1 cup** | **250 mL** |
| **Vanilla extract** | **1 tsp.** | **5 mL** |
| **Chopped walnuts** | **1 cup** | **250 mL** |
| **All-purpose flour** | **1/2 cup** | **125 mL** |
| **Baking soda** | **1/4 tsp.** | **1 mL** |
| **Salt** | **1/4 tsp.** | **1 mL** |

Beat egg in medium bowl until frothy. Add brown sugar and vanilla. Stir.

Add remaining 4 ingredients. Mix well. Spread evenly in greased 8 x 8 inch (20 x 20 cm) pan. Bake in 350°F (175°C) oven for 20 minutes. Let stand in pan on wire rack until cool. Cuts into 25 squares.

***1 square:** 76 Calories; 3.3 g Total Fat (0.4 g Mono, 2.3 g Poly, 0.4 g Sat); 9 mg Cholesterol; 11 g Carbohydrate; trace Fibre; 1 g Protein; 42 mg Sodium*

Pictured on page 54.

1. Hermit Slice, page 47
2. Peanut Krispy Squares, page 41
3. Krispy Krunch Bars, page 38
4. Festive Fruit Squares, page 43
5. Cherry Nut Bars, page 44
6. Millionaire Squares, page 45
7. Chocolate Coffee Squares, page 42
8. Lemon Slice, page 48
9. Pineapple Log, page 39
10. Nanaimo Bars, page 40
11. Marshmallow Roll, page 38

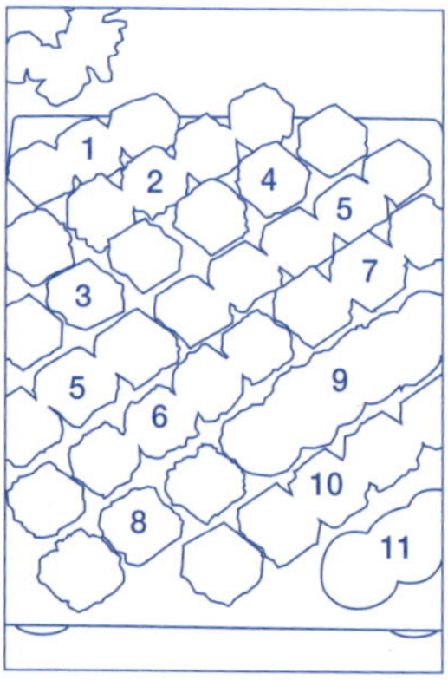

# Chocolate Nut Shortcake

*I discovered this lovely flavour combination while visiting New Zealand. Best to let these squares stand overnight before cutting.*

| | | |
|---|---|---|
| **BOTTOM LAYER** | | |
| **Egg yolks (large)** | **2** | **2** |
| **All-purpose flour** | **1 1/2 cups** | **375 mL** |
| **Brown sugar, packed** | **1/2 cup** | **125 mL** |
| **Butter (or hard margarine), softened** | **1/2 cup** | **125 mL** |
| **Baking powder** | **1 tsp.** | **5 mL** |
| **FILLING** | | |
| **Apricot jam, warmed** | **1 cup** | **250 mL** |
| **TOPPING** | | |
| **Egg whites (large)** | **2** | **2** |
| **Granulated sugar** | **3/4 cup** | **175 mL** |
| **Salted peanuts** | **3/4 cup** | **175 mL** |
| **Semi-sweet chocolate chips** | **1/2 cup** | **125 mL** |

**Bottom Layer:** Mix all 5 ingredients in large bowl until crumbly. Press firmly into ungreased 9 x 9 inch (22 x 22 cm) pan.

**Filling:** Pour warm jam over bottom layer. Spread evenly.

**Topping:** Combine all 4 ingredients in medium saucepan. Heat and stir on medium until chocolate is melted. Bring to a boil, stirring constantly. Remove from heat. Pour over filling. Bake in 350°F (175°C) oven for 30 to 35 minutes until set. Let stand in pan on wire rack until cool. Cuts into 36 squares.

***1 square:*** *126 Calories; 5.3 g Total Fat (1.0 g Mono, 0.2 g Poly, 2.6 g Sat); 18 mg Cholesterol; 19 g Carbohydrate; 0.5 g Fibre; 2 g Protein; 62 mg Sodium*

Pictured on page 71.

1. Black Bottom Slice, page 51
2. Matrimonial Squares, page 50
3. Banana Oat Squares, page 49
4. Ginger Shortbread, page 49
5. Fruit Marmalade Squares, page 57
6. Scotch Shortbread, page 56
7. Nutty Bars, page 52
8. Cranberry Oat Squares, page 56

Props courtesy of: Cherison Enterprises Inc.

# Scotch Shortbread

*A favourite and simple recipe for shortbread that always turns out great.*

| | | |
|---|---|---|
| **All-purpose flour** | **2 cups** | **500 mL** |
| **Butter** | **1 cup** | **250 mL** |
| **Icing (confectioner's) sugar** | **1/2 cup** | **125 mL** |

Mix all 3 ingredients in large bowl until crumbly. Work the mixture with your hands until it comes together to form a ball. Press firmly into ungreased 9 x 9 inch (22 x 22 cm) pan. Prick entire surface of dough with fork through to bottom of pan. Bake in 300°F (150°C) oven for about 50 minutes until just golden. Cool slightly. Cut while still warm into 36 squares.

***1 square:*** *73 Calories; 5.1 g Total Fat (1.3 g Mono, 0.2 g Poly, 3.2 g Sat); 13 mg Cholesterol; 7 g Carbohydrate; trace Fibre; 1 g Protein; 36 mg Sodium*

Pictured on page 54.

# Cranberry Oat Squares

*Sweet brown sugar combines wonderfully with tart cranberry sauce. Good served hot with ice cream.*

**CRUST**

| | | |
|---|---|---|
| **All-purpose flour** | **1 1/2 cups** | **375 mL** |
| **Quick-cooking rolled oats** | **1 1/2 cups** | **375 mL** |
| **Brown sugar, packed** | **1 cup** | **250 mL** |
| **Butter (or hard margarine), softened** | **1 cup** | **250 mL** |
| **Baking soda** | **1/4 tsp.** | **1 mL** |

**FILLING**

| | | |
|---|---|---|
| **Can of whole cranberry sauce** | **14 oz.** | **398 mL** |

**Crust:** Mix first 5 ingredients in large bowl until crumbly. Press 2/3 of mixture firmly into greased 9 x 9 inch (22 x 22 cm) pan. Reserve remaining oat mixture.

**Filling:** Spread cranberry sauce evenly over crust. Sprinkle reserved oat mixture evenly over filling. Press down gently. Bake in 350°F (175°C) oven for 35 to 40 minutes until golden brown. Let stand in pan on wire rack until cool. Cuts into 36 squares.

***1 square:*** *114 Calories; 5.3 g Total Fat (1.3 g Mono, 0.2 Poly, 3.2 g Sat); 13 mg Cholesterol; 16 g Carbohydrate; 1 g Fibre; 1 g Protein; 49 mg Sodium*

Pictured on page 54 and on back cover.

# Fruit Marmalade Squares

*This is a glistening, fruity bar. Watch that you don't overcook it or it will be too chewy.*

| | | |
|---|---|---|
| **BOTTOM LAYER** | | |
| **All-purpose flour** | **1 1/4 cups** | **300 mL** |
| **Butter (or hard margarine), softened** | **1/2 cup** | **125 mL** |
| **Granulated sugar** | **1/4 cup** | **60 mL** |
| **Egg yolk (large)** | **1** | **1** |
| **TOP LAYER** | | |
| **Large egg** | **1** | **1** |
| **Marmalade** | **1/4 cup** | **60 mL** |
| **Milk** | **2 tbsp.** | **30 mL** |
| **Chopped pitted dates** | **3/4 cup** | **175 mL** |
| **Raisins (or currants)** | **3/4 cup** | **175 mL** |
| **Chopped walnuts** | **1/2 cup** | **125 mL** |
| **Granulated sugar** | **1/4 cup** | **60 mL** |
| **Red and green glazed cherries, halved** | **18** | **18** |

**Bottom Layer:** Mix all 4 ingredients in medium bowl until crumbly. Press firmly into ungreased 9 x 9 inch (22 x 22 cm) pan. Bake in 350°F (175°C) oven for 15 minutes.

**Top Layer:** Beat egg until frothy in large bowl. Add marmalade and milk. Beat well.

Add next 4 ingredients. Stir. Spread evenly over bottom layer. Bake for about 25 minutes, until set.

Immediately press cherry halves onto hot fruit mixture, about 1 1/2 inches (3.8 cm) apart. Let stand in pan on wire rack until cool. Cuts into 36 squares.

***1 square:*** *96 Calories; 3.9 g Total Fat (0.9 g Mono, 0.9 g Poly, 2 g Sat); 18 mg Cholesterol; 15 g Carbohydrate; 1 g Fibre; 1 g Protein; 25 mg Sodium*

Pictured on page 54.

## *Paré Pointer*

*Going on a fishing trip? Better eat everything now you can get your hands on. How do you know that you will catch any fish?*

# Nutty Spice Slice

*A fruit and nut square with a mild spicy taste.*

| | | |
|---|---|---|
| Raisins (or currants) | 1/2 cup | 125 mL |
| Walnuts | 1/2 cup | 125 mL |
| Boiling water | 1/2 cup | 125 mL |
| Baking soda | 1/2 tsp. | 2 mL |
| Large egg | 1 | 1 |
| Brown sugar, packed | 1 cup | 250 mL |
| Butter (or hard margarine), softened | 1/2 cup | 125 mL |
| Vanilla extract | 1/2 tsp. | 2 mL |
| All-purpose flour | 1 1/2 cups | 375 mL |
| Ground cinnamon | 1/2 tsp. | 2 mL |
| Ground nutmeg | 1/2 tsp. | 2 mL |
| Baking powder | 1/4 tsp. | 1 mL |
| ICING | | |
| Icing (confectioner's) sugar | 1 1/2 cups | 375 mL |
| Butter (or hard margarine), softened | 3 tbsp. | 50 mL |
| Hot strong prepared coffee | 1 1/2 tbsp. | 25 mL |

Process raisins and walnuts in blender or food processor until finely chopped. Transfer to small bowl. Add boiling water and baking soda. Stir. Let stand for 5 minutes.

Beat next 4 ingredients in large bowl until smooth. Add raisin mixture. Stir well.

Combine next 4 ingredients in small bowl. Add to raisin mixture. Stir until just combined. Pour into greased 9 x 9 inch (22 x 22 cm) pan. Bake in 350°F (175°C) oven for about 40 to 45 minutes until wooden pick inserted in centre comes out clean. Let stand in pan on wire rack until cool.

**Icing:** Beat all 3 ingredients in small bowl until smooth, adding more coffee or icing sugar as necessary until spreading consistency. Spread evenly over bottom layer. Cuts into 36 squares.

***1 square:*** *111 Calories; 4.7 g Total Fat (1.1 g Mono, 0.9 g Poly, 2.4 g Sat); 15 mg Cholesterol; 17 g Carbohydrate; trace Fibre; 1 g Protein; 51 mg Sodium*

Pictured on divider page.

# Pineapple Bars

*Serve this at your next Hawaiian luau.*

| | | |
|---|---|---|
| **BOTTOM LAYER** | | |
| **All-purpose flour** | **1 1/4 cups** | **300 mL** |
| **Butter (or hard margarine), softened** | **1/2 cup** | **125 mL** |
| **Granulated sugar** | **1/4 cup** | **60 mL** |
| **SECOND LAYER** | | |
| **Large eggs** | **2** | **2** |
| **Brown sugar, packed** | **1 cup** | **250 mL** |
| **Crushed pineapple, drained and juice reserved** | **1 cup** | **250 mL** |
| **Chopped walnuts** | **1/2 cup** | **125 mL** |
| **All-purpose flour** | **2 tbsp.** | **30 mL** |
| **Almond extract** | **1/2 tsp.** | **2 mL** |
| **Baking powder** | **1/2 tsp.** | **2 mL** |
| **Salt** | **1/4 tsp.** | **1 mL** |
| **ICING** | | |
| **Icing (confectioner's) sugar** | **1 1/2 cups** | **375 mL** |
| **Butter (or hard margarine), softened** | **3 tbsp.** | **50 mL** |
| **Reserved pineapple juice** | **1 1/2 tbsp.** | **25 mL** |

**Bottom Layer:** Mix all 3 ingredients in medium bowl until crumbly. Press firmly into ungreased 9 x 9 inch (22 x 22 cm) pan. Bake in 350°F (175°C) oven for 15 minutes.

**Second Layer:** Beat eggs in large bowl until frothy. Add next 7 ingredients. Mix well. Spread evenly over bottom layer. Bake for about 30 minutes until set and browned. Let stand in pan on wire rack until cool.

**Icing:** Beat all 3 ingredients in small bowl until smooth, adding more pineapple juice or icing sugar as necessary until spreading consistency. Spread evenly over second layer. Cuts into 36 squares.

*__1 square:__ 113 Calories; 4.8 g Total Fat (1.1 g Mono, 0.9 g Poly, 2.4 g Sat); 21 mg Cholesterol; 17 g Carbohydrate; trace Fibre; 1 g Protein; 55 mg Sodium*

Pictured on page 71.

# Lemon Crunch

*Soda crackers provide a different yet delicious crunch to these squares.*

| | | |
|---|---|---|
| **BOTTOM LAYER** | | |
| **Crushed, salted soda crackers (about 38)** | **1 1/3 cups** | **325 mL** |
| **All-purpose flour** | **3/4 cup** | **175 mL** |
| **Butter (or hard margarine), softened** | **3/4 cup** | **175 mL** |
| **Granulated sugar** | **1/2 cup** | **125 mL** |
| **Medium unsweetened coconut** | **1/2 cup** | **125 mL** |
| **Baking powder** | **1 tsp.** | **5 mL** |
| **SECOND LAYER** | | |
| **Large eggs** | **3** | **3** |
| **Granulated sugar** | **1 cup** | **250 mL** |
| **Butter (or hard margarine)** | **1/4 cup** | **60 mL** |
| **Lemon juice** | **1/4 cup** | **60 mL** |
| **Grated lemon zest (see Tip)** | **2 tsp.** | **10 mL** |

**Bottom Layer:** Mix all 6 ingredients in medium bowl until crumbly. Reserve 1 cup (250 mL) for topping. Press remaining crumb mixture firmly into greased 9 x 9 inch (22 x 22 cm) pan. Bake in 350°F (175°C) oven for 15 minutes.

**Second Layer:** Whisk eggs in medium, heavy saucepan until frothy. Add remaining 4 ingredients. Heat and stir on medium for about 5 minutes, until thickened. Spread evenly over bottom layer. Sprinkle with reserved crumb mixture. Bake for about 20 minutes until golden brown. Let stand in pan on wire rack until cool. Cuts into 36 squares.

***1 square:*** *110 Calories; 6.4 g Total Fat (1.5 g Mono, 0.2 g Poly, 4.0 g Sat); 31 mg Cholesterol; 13 g Carbohydrate; trace Fibre; 1 g Protein; 85 mg Sodium*

Pictured on page 71.

*tip* When a recipe calls for grated lemon zest and juice, it's easier to grate the lemon first, then juice it. Be careful not to grate down to the pith (white part of the peel), which is bitter and best avoided.

# Butterscotch Brownies

*A chewy brownie with caramel flavour.*

| | | |
|---|---|---|
| Butter (or hard margarine), melted | 1/4 cup | 60 mL |
| Brown sugar, packed | 1 cup | 250 mL |
| Large egg | 1 | 1 |
| Vanilla extract | 1/2 tsp. | 2 mL |
| All-purpose flour | 3/4 cup | 175 mL |
| Chopped walnuts | 1/2 cup | 125 mL |
| Baking powder | 1 tsp. | 5 mL |
| Salt | 1/4 tsp. | 1 mL |
| **ICING** | | |
| Brown sugar, packed | 1/4 cup | 60 mL |
| Butter (or hard margarine) | 2 tbsp. | 30 mL |
| Milk | 2 tbsp. | 30 mL |
| Icing (confectioner's) sugar | 1 cup | 250 mL |

Melt butter in saucepan and add it to brown sugar in large bowl. Stir. Add egg and vanilla. Stir.

Add next 4 ingredients. Mix well. Spread evenly in greased 8 x 8 inch (20 x 20 cm) pan. Bake in 350°F (175°C) oven for about 30 minutes, until edges start to pull away from sides of pan and wooden pick inserted in centre comes out moist but not wet with batter. Do not overbake. Let stand in pan on wire rack until cool.

**Icing:** Combine first 3 ingredients in small saucepan. Heat and stir on medium until melted. Bring to a boil. Reduce heat to medium-low. Simmer, uncovered, for 2 minutes, stirring occasionally. Transfer to medium bowl. Cool for about 30 minutes until lukewarm.

Add icing sugar. Mix until smooth, adding more milk or icing sugar as necessary until spreading consistency. Spread evenly over brownie layer. Cuts into 25 squares.

***1 square:*** *116 Calories; 4.5 g Total Fat (1.0 g Mono, 1.2 g Poly, 1.9 g Sat); 16 mg Cholesterol; 19 g Carbohydrate; trace Fibre; 1 g Protein; 72 mg Sodium*

Pictured on page 71.

# Fruity Fruit Slice

*An attractive cherry arrangement makes this square too pretty to eat...almost.*

| | | |
|---|---|---|
| **Large eggs** | **2** | **2** |
| **Chopped pitted dates** | **1 cup** | **250 mL** |
| **Chopped walnuts** | **1 cup** | **250 mL** |
| **Diced mixed peel** | **1/2 cup** | **125 mL** |
| **Granulated sugar** | **1/2 cup** | **125 mL** |
| **All-purpose flour** | **6 tbsp.** | **100 mL** |
| **Baking powder** | **1 tsp.** | **5 mL** |
| **Salt** | **1/2 tsp.** | **2 mL** |
| **Lemon extract** | **1/4 tsp.** | **1 mL** |
| **Red and green glazed cherries, halved** | **13** | **13** |

Beat eggs in medium bowl until frothy. Add next 8 ingredients. Mix well. Transfer to greased 8 x 8 inch (20 x 20 cm) pan.

Arrange cherries, cut-side down, over top, about 1 1/2 inches (3.8 cm) apart to allow one per square. Bake in 350°F (175°C) oven for about 25 to 30 minutes until set. Let stand in pan on wire rack until cool. Cuts into 25 squares.

***1 square:*** *87 Calories; 3.5 g Total Fat (0.4 g Mono, 2.3 g Poly, 0.4 g Sat); 17 mg Cholesterol; 14 g Carbohydrate; 1 g Fibre; 2 g Protein; 76 mg Sodium*

Pictured on page 71.

## *Paré Pointer*

*Be sure to consume all the buns, butter and other extras that come with the meal in a restaurant, such as the soup and dessert. Fight inflation—don't waste a thing.*

# Caribbean Bars

*With pineapple, rum flavour and coconut, this square is a tropical treat.*

| | | |
|---|---|---|
| **BOTTOM LAYER** | | |
| All-purpose flour | 1 1/4 cups | 300 mL |
| Butter (or hard margarine), softened | 1/2 cup | 125 mL |
| Granulated sugar | 1/4 cup | 60 mL |
| **SECOND LAYER** | | |
| Large eggs | 2 | 2 |
| Brown sugar, packed | 1 cup | 250 mL |
| Medium unsweetened coconut | 1 cup | 250 mL |
| Crushed pineapple, drained and juice reserved | 1/2 cup | 125 mL |
| Chopped red glazed cherries | 1/3 cup | 75 mL |
| All-purpose flour | 2 tbsp. | 30 mL |
| Rum extract | 1 tsp. | 5 mL |
| Baking powder | 1/2 tsp. | 2 mL |
| **PINEAPPLE ICING** | | |
| Icing (confectioner's) sugar | 1 1/2 cups | 375 mL |
| Butter (or hard margarine), softened | 3 tbsp. | 50 mL |
| Reserved pineapple juice | 1 1/2 tbsp. | 25 mL |
| Rum extract | 1/2 tsp. | 2 mL |

**Bottom Layer:** Mix all 3 ingredients in medium bowl until crumbly. Press firmly into ungreased 9 x 9 inch (22 x 22 cm) pan. Bake in 350°F (175°C) oven for 15 minutes.

**Second Layer:** Beat eggs in large bowl until frothy. Add remaining 7 ingredients. Mix well. Spread evenly over bottom layer. Bake for 25 to 30 minutes until set and golden brown. Let stand in pan on wire rack until cool.

**Pineapple Icing:** Beat all 4 ingredients in medium bowl until smooth, adding more pineapple juice or icing sugar as necessary until spreading consistency. Spread evenly over second layer. Cuts into 36 squares.

***1 square:*** *119 Calories; 5.1 g Total Fat (1 g Mono, 0.2 g Poly, 3.5 g Sat); 21 mg Cholesterol; 18 g Carbohydrate; trace Fibre; 1 g Protein; 40 mg Sodium*

Pictured on page 71.

# Chocolate Cherry Slice

*A smooth chocolate bottom layer makes the difference. Make this one and see how long it lasts in your refrigerator—bet it's not long!*

| | | |
|---|---|---|
| **BOTTOM LAYER** | | |
| **Sweet chocolate baking squares, chopped (1 oz., 28g each), see Note** | **8** | **8** |
| **TOP LAYER** | | |
| **Large eggs** | **2** | **2** |
| **Granulated sugar** | **1/2 cup** | **125 mL** |
| **Medium unsweetened coconut** | **1 1/2 cups** | **375 mL** |
| **Chopped red glazed cherries** | **1/4 cup** | **60 mL** |
| **Icing (confectioner's) sugar, for dusting** | | |

**Bottom Layer:** Heat chocolate in small, heavy saucepan on lowest heat, stirring often, until chocolate is almost melted. Remove from heat. Stir until smooth. Spread evenly in greased 8 x 8 inch (20 x 20 cm) pan. Chill until firm.

**Top Layer:** Beat eggs and sugar in medium bowl. Fold in coconut and cherries. Spread evenly over bottom layer. Bake in 350°F (175°C) oven for about 25 to 30 minutes until set and golden. Let stand in pan on wire rack until cool.

Just before serving, dust with icing sugar. Cuts into 25 squares.

***1 square:** 96 Calories; 4.6 g Total Fat (0.6 g Mono, 0.1 g Poly, 3.4 g Sat); 17 mg Cholesterol; 14 g Carbohydrate; 1 g Fibre; 1 g Protein; 9 mg Sodium*

Pictured on page 71.

**Note:** You can use 1 1/3 cups (325 mL) chocolate chips in place of the chocolate baking squares in this recipe.

### Paré Pointer

*Don't eat like a rabbit with all that so-called rabbit food. Bigger animals eat them for dinner. Defend yourself. Eat lots.*

# Caramel Slice

*An exceptionally delicious square for caramel and nut lovers.*

| | | |
|---|---|---|
| **BOTTOM LAYER** | | |
| **Butter (or hard margarine)** | **1/4 cup** | **60 mL** |
| **Brown sugar, packed** | **1 cup** | **250 mL** |
| **Large eggs, fork-beaten** | **2** | **2** |
| **Medium unsweetened coconut** | **1 cup** | **250 mL** |
| **All-purpose flour** | **3/4 cup** | **175 mL** |
| **Chopped walnuts** | **1/2 cup** | **125 mL** |
| **Baking powder** | **1 tsp.** | **5 mL** |
| **Salt** | **1/4 tsp.** | **1 mL** |
| **CARAMEL ICING** | | |
| **Brown sugar, packed** | **1/2 cup** | **125 mL** |
| **Butter (or hard margarine)** | **1/4 cup** | **60 mL** |
| **Milk** | **2 tbsp.** | **30 mL** |
| **Icing (confectioner's) sugar** | **1 cup** | **250 mL** |

**Bottom Layer:** Melt butter in large saucepan on medium. Remove from heat. Add brown sugar. Stir. Add eggs. Stir. Add next 5 ingredients. Stir well. Spread evenly in greased 9 x 9 inch (22 x 22 cm) pan. Bake in 350°F (175°C) oven for 20 to 25 minutes until set and edges are golden. Let stand in pan on wire rack until cool.

**Caramel Icing:** Combine first 3 ingredients in small saucepan. Heat and stir on medium until melted. Bring to a boil. Reduce heat to medium-low. Simmer, uncovered, for 2 minutes, stirring occasionally. Transfer to medium bowl. Cool for about 30 minutes until lukewarm.

Add icing sugar. Beat until light and creamy, adding more milk or icing sugar as necessary until spreading consistency. Spread evenly over bottom layer. Cuts into 36 squares.

***1 square:*** *107 Calories; 5.2 g Total Fat (0.9 g Mono, 0.9 g Poly, 3.0 g Sat); 19 mg Cholesterol; 15 g Carbohydrate; trace Fibre; 1 g Protein; 58 mg Sodium*

Pictured on page 71.

### *Paré Pointer*

*Those two are always cooking up something but rarely on the stove.*

# Banana Bars

*There aren't many delicious squares with bananas in them, but this one more than makes the cut.*

| | | |
|---|---|---|
| **Butter (or hard margarine), softened** | **1/4 cup** | **60 mL** |
| **Brown sugar, packed** | **1/2 cup** | **125 mL** |
| **Large egg** | **1** | **1** |
| **Vanilla extract** | **1/2 tsp.** | **2 mL** |
| **Mashed banana (about 1 medium)** | **1/2 cup** | **125 mL** |
| **Apricot jam** | **1/3 cup** | **75 mL** |
| **Lemon juice** | **1 tsp.** | **5 mL** |
| **All-purpose flour** | **1 cup** | **250 mL** |
| **Baking powder** | **1/2 tsp.** | **2 mL** |
| **Chopped walnuts** | **1/4 cup** | **60 mL** |
| **Salt** | **1/4 tsp.** | **1 mL** |
| **Apricot jam, strained through fine sieve** | **1/4 cup** | **60 mL** |
| **Ground walnuts** | **1/4 cup** | **60 mL** |

Beat butter and brown sugar in large bowl. Add egg and vanilla. Beat until light and fluffy.

Add next 3 ingredients. Stir.

Combine next 4 ingredients in small bowl. Add to egg mixture. Stir well. Spread evenly in greased 9 x 9 inch (22 x 22 cm) pan. Bake in 350°F (175°C) oven for 25 to 30 minutes until wooden pick inserted in centre comes out clean.

Immediately spread second amount of jam evenly over top. Sprinkle with ground walnuts. Let stand in pan on wire rack until cool. Cuts into 36 squares.

***1 square:*** *61 Calories; 2.3 g Total Fat (0.5 g Mono, 0.7 g Poly, 1.0 g Sat); 9 mg Cholesterol; 10 g Carbohydrate; trace Fibre; 1 g Protein; 38 mg Sodium*

Pictured on page 72.

# Festive Fruitcake

*The next best thing to a Christmas cake, and it bakes in a fraction of the time.*

| | | |
|---|---|---|
| All-purpose flour | 1/4 cup | 60 mL |
| Chopped mixed glazed fruit | 2/3 cup | 150 mL |
| Butter (or hard margarine), softened | 1/2 cup | 125 mL |
| Granulated sugar | 1/2 cup | 125 mL |
| Large egg | 1 | 1 |
| Frozen concentrated orange juice, thawed | 2 tbsp. | 30 mL |
| Grated orange zest | 1 tsp. | 5 mL |
| Almond extract | 1/4 tsp. | 1 mL |
| All-purpose flour | 1 1/2 cups | 375 mL |
| Baking soda | 1/2 tsp. | 2 mL |
| Salt | 1/4 tsp. | 1 mL |
| Chopped walnuts | 1/2 cup | 125 mL |
| **ORANGE ICING** | | |
| Icing (confectioner's) sugar | 1 1/2 cups | 375 mL |
| Butter (or hard margarine), softened | 3 tbsp. | 50 mL |
| Orange juice | 1 1/2 tbsp. | 25 mL |

Toss first amount of flour with glazed fruit in small bowl until coated.

Beat butter and sugar in large bowl. Add next 4 ingredients. Beat well.

Combine next 3 ingredients in small bowl. Add to orange mixture. Mix well. Fold in walnuts and fruit mixture. Spread evenly in greased 9 x 9 inch (22 x 22 cm) pan. Bake in 350°F (175°C) oven for about 20 minutes until edges start to pull away from sides of pan. Let stand in pan on wire rack until cool.

**Orange Icing:** Beat all 3 ingredients in medium bowl until smooth, adding more orange juice or icing sugar as necessary until spreading consistency. Spread evenly over fruitcake layer. Cuts into 36 squares.

***1 square:*** *109 Calories; 4.7 g Total Fat (1.1 g Mono, 0.9 g Poly, 2.3 g Sat); 15 mg Cholesterol; 16 g Carbohydrate; trace Fibre; 1 g Protein; 64 mg Sodium*

Pictured on page 72.

# Marble Squares

*This takes a bit more time to make, but anything so rich is bound to be worthwhile!*

| | | |
|---|---|---|
| **Large eggs** | **2** | **2** |
| **Brown sugar, packed** | **1 cup** | **250 mL** |
| **All-purpose flour** | **3/4 cup** | **175 mL** |
| **Granulated sugar** | **1/4 cup** | **60 mL** |
| **Vanilla extract** | **1 tsp.** | **5 mL** |
| **Baking powder** | **1/2 tsp.** | **2 mL** |
| **Salt** | **1/8 tsp.** | **0.5 mL** |
| **Medium unsweetened coconut** | **1/2 cup** | **125 mL** |
| **Unsweetened chocolate baking square (1 oz., 28 g), chopped** | **1** | **1** |
| **Butter (or hard margarine)** | **1 tbsp.** | **15 mL** |
| **Chopped walnuts** | **1/4 cup** | **60 mL** |
| **Large marshmallows, cut in half** | **18** | **18** |
| **ICING** | | |
| **Icing (confectioner's) sugar** | **1 1/3 cups** | **325 mL** |
| **Butter (or hard margarine), softened** | **2 tbsp.** | **30 mL** |
| **Cocoa, sifted if lumpy** | **1/3 cup** | **75 mL** |
| **Water** | **1 1/2 tbsp.** | **25 mL** |

Beat eggs in large bowl until frothy. Add next 6 ingredients. Stir well. Divide batter into 2 portions.

Add coconut to one portion. Mix well. Spread evenly in greased 9 x 9 inch (22 x 22 cm) pan.

Heat chocolate and butter in small, heavy saucepan on lowest heat, stirring often, until chocolate is almost melted. Remove from heat. Stir until smooth. Add walnuts. Add to remaining batter. Mix well. Spread evenly over coconut layer. Bake in 350°F (175°C) oven for 30 minutes.

Arrange marshmallow halves in 6 rows over chocolate layer. Bake for 2 minutes. Carefully spread into even layer.

**Icing:** Beat all 4 ingredients in medium bowl until smooth, adding more water or icing sugar as necessary until spreading consistency. Spread evenly over warm marshmallow layer. Let stand in pan on wire rack until cool. Cuts into 36 squares.

***1 square:** 94 Calories; 2.6 g Total Fat (0.4 g Mono, 0.5 g Poly, 1.4 g Sat); 14 mg Cholesterol; 17 g Carbohydrate; trace Fibre; 1 g Protein; 32 mg Sodium*

Pictured on page 72.

# Pineapple Brownies

*The addition of pineapple makes these brownies delectably tender and moist.*

| | | |
|---|---|---|
| **Unsweetened chocolate baking squares, chopped (1 oz., 28 g, each)** | **2** | **2** |
| **Butter (or hard margarine)** | **1/2 cup** | **125 mL** |
| **Large eggs** | **2** | **2** |
| **Granulated sugar** | **1 cup** | **250 mL** |
| **Vanilla extract** | **1/2 tsp.** | **2 mL** |
| **Crushed pineapple, drained and juice reserved** | **1/2 cup** | **125 mL** |
| **All-purpose flour** | **1 cup** | **250 mL** |
| **Chopped walnuts** | **1/2 cup** | **125 mL** |
| **Baking powder** | **1/2 tsp.** | **2 mL** |
| **Salt** | **1/2 tsp.** | **2 mL** |
| **Baking soda** | **1/4 tsp.** | **1 mL** |
| **ICING** | | |
| **Icing (confectioner's) sugar** | **1 1/2 cups** | **375 mL** |
| **Butter (or hard margarine), softened** | **3 tbsp.** | **50 mL** |
| **Reserved pineapple juice** | **1 1/2 tbsp.** | **25 mL** |

Heat chocolate and butter in small, heavy saucepan on lowest heat, stirring often, until chocolate is almost melted. Remove from heat. Stir until smooth.

Beat next 3 ingredients in large bowl until combined. Add pineapple and chocolate mixture. Stir.

Combine next 5 ingredients in small bowl. Add to pineapple mixture. Stir well. Spread evenly in greased 9 x 9 inch (22 x 22 cm) pan. Bake in 350°F (175°C) oven for about 30 minutes, until wooden pick inserted in centre comes out moist but not wet with batter. Do not overbake. Let stand in pan on wire rack until cool.

**Icing:** Beat all 3 ingredients in small bowl until smooth, adding more pineapple juice or icing sugar as necessary until spreading consistency. Spread evenly over brownie layer. Cuts into 36 squares.

***1 square:*** *107 Calories; 5.1 g Total Fat (1.1 g Mono, 0.9 g Poly, 2.5 g Sat); 21 mg Cholesterol; 15 g Carbohydrate; trace Fibre; 1 g Protein; 77 mg Sodium*

Pictured on page 72.

# Apple Squares

*A cake-like square with little pits made where the apple shrinks when baking.*

| | | |
|---|---|---|
| **Large eggs** | **2** | **2** |
| **All-purpose flour** | **1 cup** | **250 mL** |
| **Granulated sugar** | **1 cup** | **250 mL** |
| **Butter (or hard margarine), softened** | **6 tbsp.** | **100 mL** |
| **Baking soda** | **1 tsp.** | **5 mL** |
| **Vanilla extract** | **1 tsp.** | **5 mL** |
| **Ground cinnamon** | **1/4 tsp.** | **1 mL** |
| **Chopped, peeled cooking apple (such as McIntosh)** | **2 cups** | **500 mL** |
| **Chopped walnuts** | **1/2 cup** | **125 mL** |
| **Icing (confectioner's) sugar, for dusting** | | |

Beat first 7 ingredients in large bowl until smooth.

Add apple and walnuts. Stir well. Spread evenly in greased 9 x 9 inch (22 x 22 cm) pan. Bake in 350°F (175°C) oven for about 45 minutes until wooden pick inserted in centre comes out clean. Let stand in pan on wire rack until cool.

Just before serving, dust with icing sugar. Cuts into 36 squares.

***1 square:*** *69 Calories; 3.2 g Total Fat (0.6 g Mono, 0.9 g Poly, 1.4 g Sat); 17 mg Cholesterol; 9 g Carbohydrate; trace Fibre; 1 g Protein; 52 mg Sodium*

Pictured on page 72.

1. Pineapple Bars, page 59
2. Chocolate Nut Shortcake, page 55
3. Fruity Fruit Slice, page 62
4. Caramel Slice, page 65
5. Butterscotch Brownies, page 61
6. Lemon Crunch, page 60
7. Chocolate Cherry Slice, page 64
8. Caribbean Bars, page 63

Props courtesy of: Stokes

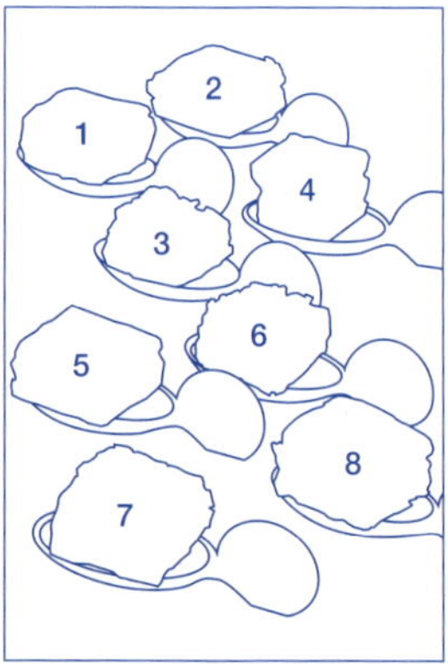

# Graham Cracker Chew

*Once you get the dates cut up, this is one of the fastest square recipes around. When unexpected company is coming, you can have this in the oven in no time.*

| | | |
|---|---|---|
| **Large eggs** | **2** | **2** |
| **Graham cracker crumbs** | **1 1/2 cups** | **375 mL** |
| **Brown sugar, packed** | **1 cup** | **250 mL** |
| **Chopped pitted dates** | **1 cup** | **250 mL** |
| **Chopped walnuts** | **1 cup** | **250 mL** |
| **Baking powder** | **1 tsp.** | **5 mL** |

**ICING**

| | | |
|---|---|---|
| **Icing (confectioner's) sugar** | **1 1/2 cups** | **375 mL** |
| **Cocoa, sifted if lumpy** | **1/3 cup** | **75 mL** |
| **Butter (or hard margarine), softened** | **3 tbsp.** | **50 mL** |
| **Hot strong prepared coffee** | **1 1/2 tbsp.** | **25 mL** |

Beat eggs in large bowl until frothy. Add next 5 ingredients. Mix well. Press firmly into greased 9 x 9 inch (22 x 22 cm) pan. Bake in 350°F (175°C) oven for about 25 minutes until set. Let stand in pan on wire rack until cool.

**Icing:** Beat all 4 ingredients in medium bowl until smooth, adding more coffee or icing sugar as necessary until spreading consistency. Spread evenly over bottom layer. Cuts into 36 squares.

***1 square:*** *108 Calories; 3.8 g Total Fat (0.7 g Mono, 1.7 g Poly, 0.9 g Sat); 14 mg Cholesterol; 18 g Carbohydrate; 1 g Fibre; 1 g Protein; 49 mg Sodium*

Pictured on page 89.

1. Double Brownies, page 76
2. Pineapple Brownies, page 69
3. Marble Squares, page 68
4. Marzipan Bars, page 74
5. Apple Squares, page 70
6. Banana Bars, page 66
7. Cheese Apple Squares, page 77
8. Festive Fruitcake, page 67
9. Mincemeat Squares, page 82

# Marzipan Bars

*A pretty, festive, almond-flavoured square. It takes a little longer than usual to put in the pan, but the end result is well worth it.*

| | | |
|---|---|---|
| **BOTTOM LAYER** | | |
| Pastry for 9 inch (22 cm) pie shell | | |
| Raspberry jam | 1/4 cup | 60 mL |
| **MIDDLE LAYER** | | |
| Butter (or hard margarine), softened | 1/2 cup | 125 mL |
| Granulated sugar | 2/3 cup | 150 mL |
| Large eggs | 2 | 2 |
| Rice flour | 2/3 cup | 150 mL |
| Salt | 1/4 tsp. | 1 mL |
| Drops of red liquid food colouring | 1 – 3 | 1 – 3 |
| Drops of green liquid food colouring | 1 – 3 | 1 – 3 |
| **ALMOND ICING** | | |
| Icing (confectioner's) sugar | 1 1/2 cups | 375 mL |
| Butter (or hard margarine), softened | 3 tbsp. | 50 mL |
| Milk | 1 1/2 tbsp. | 25 mL |
| Almond extract | 1 tsp. | 5 mL |

**Bottom Layer:** Press pastry into bottom of ungreased 9 x 9 inch (22 x 22 cm) pan. Spread jam evenly over top

**Middle Layer:** Beat butter and sugar in medium bowl. Add eggs, 1 at a time, beating well after each addition until fluffy. Stir in rice flour and salt. Divide batter into 2 equal portions.

Add red food colouring to 1 portion. Mix well. Add green food colouring to remaining portion. Mix well. Drop by rounded teaspoonfuls, alternating colours, over bottom layer to make a checkerboard pattern. It will spread flat as it bakes. Bake on bottom rack in 375°F (190°C) oven for about 25 minutes until golden. Let stand in pan on wire rack until cool.

**Almond Icing:** Beat all 4 ingredients in small bowl until smooth, adding more milk or icing sugar as necessary until spreading consistency. Spread evenly over middle layer. Cuts into 36 squares.

***1 square:** 117 Calories; 5.4 g Total Fat (0.9 g Mono, 0.1 g Poly, 3.0 g Sat); 22 mg Cholesterol; 17 g Carbohydrate; trace Fibre; 1 g Protein; 67 mg Sodium*

Pictured on page 72.

# Apricot Zings

*This popular square sells well at bake sales.*

| | | |
|---|---|---|
| **BOTTOM LAYER** | | |
| Butter (or hard margarine), melted | 3/4 cup | 175 mL |
| All-purpose flour | 1 cup | 250 mL |
| Brown sugar, packed | 1 cup | 250 mL |
| Graham cracker crumbs | 1 cup | 250 mL |
| Medium unsweetened coconut | 1/2 cup | 125 mL |
| Salt | 1/2 tsp. | 2 mL |
| **FILLING** | | |
| Dried apricots | 1 cup | 250 mL |
| Water, to cover | | |
| Large eggs | 2 | 2 |
| Brown sugar, packed | 1 cup | 250 mL |
| Lemon juice | 1 tbsp. | 15 mL |
| All-purpose flour | 1/3 cup | 75 mL |
| Baking powder | 1/2 tsp. | 2 mL |
| Salt | 1/4 tsp. | 1 mL |

**Bottom Layer:** Melt butter in medium saucepan. Combine next 5 ingredients in medium bowl. Add melted butter. Mix well. Reserve 1 cup (250 mL) crumb mixture in small bowl. Press remaining mixture firmly into ungreased 9 x 9 inch (22 x 22 cm) pan. Bake in 350°F (175°C) oven for 10 minutes.

**Filling:** Place apricots in small saucepan. Add enough water to cover. Bring to a boil on medium. Reduce heat to medium-low. Simmer, uncovered, for about 15 minutes, until apricots are softened. Drain well. Chop.

Beat eggs in medium bowl until frothy. Add brown sugar and lemon juice. Stir well.

Combine remaining 3 ingredients in small bowl. Add to egg mixture. Stir. Add apricot. Stir well. Spread evenly over bottom layer. Sprinkle with reserved crumb mixture. Bake for 30 to 35 minutes until golden. Let stand in pan on wire rack until cool. Cuts into 36 squares.

***1 square:** 125 Calories; 4.9 g Total Fat (1.1 g Mono, 0.2 g Poly, 3.1 g Sat); 22 mg Cholesterol; 20 g Carbohydrate; 1 g Fibre; 1 g Protein; 108 mg Sodium*

Pictured on page 89.

# Double Brownies

*Chocolate or butterscotch brownies? Why not have both!*

| | | |
|---|---|---|
| **CHOCOLATE LAYER** | | |
| Large eggs | 2 | 2 |
| Granulated sugar | 1 cup | 250 mL |
| All-purpose flour | 3/4 cup | 175 mL |
| Chopped walnuts | 1/2 cup | 125 mL |
| Salt | 1/8 tsp. | 0.5 mL |
| Butter (or hard margarine) | 1/2 cup | 125 mL |
| Cocoa, sifted if lumpy | 1/4 cup | 60 mL |
| **BUTTERSCOTCH LAYER** | | |
| Butter (or hard margarine), softened | 1/2 cup | 125 mL |
| Brown sugar, packed | 1 1/2 cups | 375 mL |
| Large eggs | 2 | 2 |
| Vanilla extract | 2 tsp. | 10 mL |
| All-purpose flour | 1 1/2 cups | 375 mL |
| Chopped walnuts | 1/2 cup | 125 mL |
| Salt | 1/4 tsp. | 1 mL |
| **ICING** | | |
| Brown sugar, packed | 1/2 cup | 125 mL |
| Butter (or hard margarine) | 1/4 cup | 60 mL |
| Milk | 3 tbsp. | 50 mL |
| Icing (confectioner's) sugar | 1 1/2 cups | 375 mL |
| Semi-sweet chocolate chips | 2/3 cup | 150 mL |
| Butter (or hard margarine) | 1 tbsp. | 15 mL |

**Chocolate Layer:** Beat eggs in large bowl until frothy. Add next 4 ingredients. Stir.

Heat butter and cocoa in small saucepan on low until smooth. Add to egg mixture. Mix well. Spread evenly in greased 9 x 13 inch (22 x 33 cm) pan. Set aside.

**Butterscotch Layer:** Beat butter and brown sugar in separate large bowl. Add eggs and vanilla. Beat well. Add remaining 3 ingredients. Stir. Drop by rounded teaspoonfuls, in dabs here and there, over chocolate layer. Spread evenly. Bake in 350°F (175°C) oven for about 35 minutes until edges start

*(continued on next page)*

to pull away from sides of pan and wooden pick inserted in centre comes out moist but not wet with batter. Do not overbake. Let stand in pan on wire rack until cool.

**Icing:** Combine first 3 ingredients in small saucepan. Heat and stir on medium until melted. Bring to a boil. Reduce heat to medium-low. Simmer, uncovered, for 2 minutes, stirring occasionally. Transfer to medium bowl. Cool for about 30 minutes until lukewarm.

Add icing sugar. Beat until light and creamy, adding more milk or icing sugar as necessary until spreading consistency. Spread evenly over butterscotch layer.

Heat chocolate chips and butter in small, heavy saucepan on lowest heat, stirring often, until chocolate is almost melted. Remove from heat. Stir until smooth. Drizzle over icing. Cuts into 54 squares.

***1 square:** 146 Calories; 6.9 g Total Fat (1.6 g Mono, 1.2 g Poly, 3.4 g Sat); 28 mg Cholesterol; 21 g Carbohydrate; trace Fibre; 2 g Protein; 56 mg Sodium*

Pictured on page 72.

# Cheese Apple Squares

*This classic flavour combination makes a lovely square for lunches.*

| | | |
|---|---|---|
| **All-purpose flour** | **1 1/2 cups** | **375 mL** |
| **Butter (or hard margarine), softened** | **1/2 cup** | **125 mL** |
| **Granulated sugar** | **2 tbsp.** | **30 mL** |
| **Baking powder** | **1 tsp.** | **5 mL** |
| **Grated medium Cheddar cheese** | **1 cup** | **250 mL** |
| **Apple jelly, stirred** | **1 cup** | **250 mL** |

Mix first 4 ingredients in medium bowl until crumbly.

Add cheese. Stir. Reserve 1 cup (250 mL) in small bowl. Press remaining cheese mixture firmly into greased 8 x 8 inch (20 x 20 cm) pan. Bake in 350°F (175°C) oven for 15 minutes.

Spread jelly evenly over top. Sprinkle with reserved crumb mixture. Bake for about 20 minutes until golden. Let stand in pan on wire rack until cool. Cuts into 25 squares.

***1 square:** 111 Calories; 5.1 g Total Fat (1.4 g Mono, 0.2 g Poly, 3.3 g Sat); 14 mg Cholesterol; 15 g Carbohydrate; trace Fibre; 2 g Protein; 76 mg Sodium*

Pictured on page 72.

# Cherry Triangles

*This unique square has only a hint of sweetness. The centre ribbon of red makes it quite an eye-catcher.*

| | | |
|---|---|---|
| Milk | 2/3 cup | 150 mL |
| Granulated sugar | 1 tsp. | 5 mL |
| Envelope of active dry yeast (or 2 1/4 tsp., 11 mL) | 1/4 oz. | 8 g |
| Butter (or hard margarine), softened | 1 cup | 250 mL |
| All-purpose flour | 2 3/4 cups | 675 mL |
| Egg yolks (large), fork-beaten | 4 | 4 |
| Minute tapioca | 2 tbsp. | 30 mL |
| Can of cherry pie filling | 19 oz. | 540 mL |
| TOPPING | | |
| Icing (confectioner's) sugar | 1 1/2 cups | 375 mL |
| Butter (or hard margarine), softened | 3 tbsp. | 50 mL |
| Water | 1 1/2 tbsp. | 25 mL |
| Vanilla extract | 1/2 tsp. | 2 mL |
| Finely chopped walnuts | 2 tbsp. | 30 mL |
| Chopped red glazed cherries (optional) | 2 tbsp. | 30 mL |

Combine milk and sugar in small saucepan. Heat and stir on medium until warm and sugar is dissolved. Pour into small bowl. Let stand for about 5 minutes until lukewarm.

Sprinkle yeast over top. Let stand for 10 minutes. Stir until yeast is dissolved.

Cut butter into flour in large bowl until crumbly. Add egg yolks and yeast mixture. Mix until smooth dough forms. Turn out onto lightly floured surface. Knead 8 to 10 times until smooth. Divide dough into 2 portions. Roll out one portion into 9 x 13 inch (22 x 33 cm) rectangle. Press into bottom of greased 9 x 13 inch (22 x 33 cm) pan.

Stir tapioca into pie filling. Spread evenly over dough. Roll out remaining dough portion into 9 x 13 inch (22 x 33 cm) rectangle. Carefully place over pie filling. Bake in 350°F (175°C) oven for about 45 minutes until golden. Let stand in pan on wire rack until cool.

*(continued on next page)*

**Topping:** Beat first 4 ingredients in medium bowl until smooth, adding more water or icing sugar as necessary until spreading consistency. Spread evenly over top pastry layer.

Sprinkle with walnuts and cherries. Cut into 24 squares. Cut squares in half diagonally to make 48 triangles.

***1 triangle:*** *101 Calories; 5.1 g Total Fat (1.4 g Mono, 0.4 g Poly, 3.0 g Sat); 29 mg Cholesterol; 13 g Carbohydrate; trace Fibre; 1 g Protein; 37 mg Sodium*

Pictured on page 89.

# Gumdrop Bars

*Here is a fun substitute for mixed glazed fruit—gumdrop candies! Bars have a caramel flavour.*

| | | |
|---|---|---|
| **Butter (or hard margarine), softened** | 1/3 cup | 75 mL |
| **Brown sugar, packed** | 1/3 cup | 75 mL |
| **Granulated sugar** | 1/2 cup | 125 mL |
| **Large eggs** | 2 | 2 |
| **All-purpose flour** | 1 cup | 250 mL |
| **Quick-cooking rolled oats** | 1 cup | 250 mL |
| **Cut up gumdrops (no black)** | 1/2 cup | 125 mL |
| **Medium unsweetened coconut** | 1/2 cup | 125 mL |
| **Baking powder** | 1/2 tsp. | 2 mL |
| **Baking soda** | 1/2 tsp. | 2 mL |
| **Vanilla extract** | 1/2 tsp. | 2 mL |
| **Salt** | 1/4 tsp. | 1 mL |

**Icing (confectioner's) sugar, for dusting**

Beat first 3 ingredients in large bowl. Add eggs, 1 at a time, beating well after each addition.

Add next 8 ingredients. Mix well. Press firmly into greased 9 x 9 inch (22 x 22 cm) pan. Bake in 350° (175°C) oven for 25 to 30 minutes until golden. Let stand in pan on wire rack until cool.

Just before serving, dust with icing sugar. Cuts into 36 squares.

***1 square:*** *75 Calories; 2.8 g Total Fat (0.5 g Mono, 0.1 g Poly, 1.7 g Sat); 16 mg Cholesterol; 12 g Carbohydrate; trace Fibre; 1 g Protein; 59 mg Sodium*

Pictured on divider page.

# Cream Cheese Brownies

*Rich cream cheese and super-sweet cherries provide a tasty take on brownies.*

| | | |
|---|---|---|
| Large egg | 1 | 1 |
| Block of cream cheese, softened | 4 oz. | 125 g |
| Granulated sugar | 1/2 cup | 125 mL |
| All-purpose flour | 2 tbsp. | 30 mL |
| Chopped maraschino cherries, well drained | 1/2 cup | 125 mL |
| **BROWNIE LAYER** | | |
| Large eggs | 2 | 2 |
| Granulated sugar | 1 cup | 250 mL |
| All-purpose flour | 3/4 cup | 175 mL |
| Chopped walnuts | 1/2 cup | 125 mL |
| Salt | 1/8 tsp. | 0.5 mL |
| Butter (or hard margarine), cut up | 1/2 cup | 125 mL |
| Cocoa, sifted if lumpy | 1/4 cup | 60 mL |
| **CHOCOLATE COFFEE ICING** | | |
| Icing (confectioner's) sugar | 1 1/3 cups | 325 mL |
| Cocoa, sifted if lumpy | 1/3 cup | 75 mL |
| Butter (or hard margarine), softened | 3 tbsp. | 50 mL |
| Hot strong prepared coffee | 1 1/2 tbsp. | 25 mL |

Beat egg and cream cheese in medium bowl until smooth. Combine sugar and flour in small bowl. Add to cream cheese mixture, 2 tbsp. (30 mL) at a time while beating, until smooth. Add cherries. Stir. Set aside.

**Brownie Layer:** Beat eggs in separate medium bowl until frothy. Add next 4 ingredients. Stir.

Combine butter and cocoa in small saucepan. Heat and stir on low until just melted. Add to egg mixture. Stir well. Spread 2/3 of brownie mixture evenly in greased 9 x 9 inch (22 x 22 cm) pan. Drop spoonfuls of cream cheese mixture over top, using 1 tbsp. (15 mL) for each. Drop spoonfuls of remaining brownie mixture over top, using 1/2 tsp. (2 mL) for each. Mixtures will look patchy in pan. Bake in 350°F (175°C) oven for 30 to 35 minutes until edges start to pull away from sides of pan. Let stand in pan on wire rack until cooled completely.

**Chocolate Coffee Icing:** Beat all 4 ingredients in small bowl until smooth, adding more coffee or icing sugar as necessary until spreading consistency.

*(continued on next page)*

Spread evenly over brownies. Cuts into 25 squares.

***1 square:*** *184 Calories; 8.8 g Total Fat (1.5 g Mono, 1.3 g Poly, 4.6 g Sat); 43.6 mg Cholesterol; 25 g Carbohydrate; 1 g Fibre; 2 g Protein; 70 mg Sodium*

Pictured on divider page.

# Five Cup Slice

*A quick and easy bar that everyone likes.*

| | | |
|---|---|---|
| **Can of sweetened condensed milk** | **11 oz.** | **300 mL** |
| **Medium unsweetened coconut** | **1 1/4 cups** | **300 mL** |
| **Raisins (or currants) (see Note)** | **1 1/4 cups** | **300 mL** |
| **Semi-sweet chocolate chips** | **1 1/4 cups** | **300 mL** |
| **Unsalted peanuts (see Note)** | **1 1/4 cups** | **300 mL** |

Combine all 5 ingredients in large bowl. Spread evenly in greased 9 x 9 inch (22 x 22 cm) pan. Bake in 350°F (175°C) oven for 25 to 30 minutes until starting to turn golden. Let stand in pan on wire rack until cool. Cuts into 36 squares.

***1 square:*** *122 Calories; 6.6 g Total Fat (1.9 g Mono, 0.9 g Poly, 3.3 g Sat); 2 mg Cholesterol; 15 g Carbohydrate; 1 g Fibre; 2 g Protein; 14 mg Sodium*

Pictured on page 89.

**Note:** If you prefer, you could chop the raisins and peanuts for better distribution.

# Quick Hurry Bars

*These whip up quicker than quick.*

| | | |
|---|---|---|
| **Graham cracker crumbs** | **2 cups** | **500 mL** |
| **Flaked coconut** | **1 1/3 cups** | **325 mL** |
| **Chopped walnuts** | **1 cup** | **250 mL** |
| **Can of sweetened condensed milk** | **11 oz.** | **300 mL** |

Combine first 3 ingredients in medium bowl. Add condensed milk. Stir well. Spread evenly in well-greased 8 x 8 inch (20 x 20 cm) pan. Bake in 350°F (175°C) oven for about 40 minutes until golden. Let stand in pan on wire rack until cool. Cuts into 25 squares.

***1 square:*** *121 Calories; 6.1 g Total Fat (0.8 g Mono, 2.5 g Poly, 2.2 g Sat); 3 mg Cholesterol; 15 g Carbohydrate; 1 g Fibre; 2 g Protein; 66 mg Sodium*

Pictured on page 89.

# Mincemeat Squares

*This is especially good if you have any homemade mincemeat. It has a slightly spicy taste and is very moist.*

| | | |
|---|---|---|
| **All-purpose flour** | **1 1/2 cups** | **375 mL** |
| **Butter (or hard margarine), softened** | **3/4 cup** | **175 mL** |
| **Brown sugar, packed** | **1/2 cup** | **125 mL** |
| **Quick-cooking rolled oats** | **1/2 cup** | **125 mL** |
| **Mincemeat** | **1 cup** | **250 mL** |
| **Icing (confectioner's) sugar, for dusting** | | |

Mix first 4 ingredients in medium bowl until crumbly. Press 2/3 of crumb mixture firmly into ungreased 9 x 9 inch (22 x 22 cm) pan. Reserve remaining crumb mixture.

Process mincemeat in blender until smooth. Spread evenly over crumb mixture. Sprinkle with reserved crumb mixture. Press down gently. Bake in 350°F (175°C) oven for 25 to 30 minutes until golden brown. Let stand in pan on wire rack until cool.

Just before serving, dust with icing sugar. Cuts into 36 squares.

***1 square:*** *79 Calories; 3.9 g Total Fat (1.0 g Mono, 0.1 g Poly, 2.4 g Sat); 10 mg Cholesterol; 11 g Carbohydrate; trace Fibre; 1 g Protein; 43 mg Sodium*

Pictured on page 72.

# Peanut Butter Bars

*The addition of peanut butter livens up this simple shortbread.*

| | | |
|---|---|---|
| **Brown sugar, packed** | **3/4 cup** | **175 mL** |
| **Butter (or hard margarine), softened** | **1/2 cup** | **125 mL** |
| **Smooth peanut butter** | **1/4 cup** | **60 mL** |
| **Large egg** | **1** | **1** |
| **Vanilla extract** | **1 tsp.** | **5 mL** |
| **All-purpose flour** | **1 3/4 cups** | **425 mL** |
| **CHOCOLATE PEANUT GLAZE** | | |
| **Semi-sweet chocolate chips** | **2/3 cup** | **150 mL** |
| **Smooth peanut butter** | **3 tbsp.** | **50 mL** |

*(continued on next page)*

Beat first 5 ingredients in large bowl until smooth. Add flour. Mix well. Press into greased 9 x 9 inch (22 x 22 cm) pan. Bake in 350°F (150°C) oven for about 20 to 25 minutes until golden. Let stand in pan on wire rack until cool.

**Chocolate Peanut Glaze:** Heat chocolate chips and peanut butter in small, heavy saucepan on lowest heat, stirring often, until chocolate is almost melted. Remove from heat. Stir until smooth. Spread evenly over bottom layer. Cuts into 36 squares.

*__1 square:__ 95 Calories; 5.2 g Total Fat (1.0 g Mono, 0.1 g Poly, 2.5 g Sat); 12.7 mg Cholesterol; 11.4 g Carbohydrate; trace Fibre; 2 g Protein; 36 mg Sodium*

Pictured on divider page.

# Fruit Cocktail Bars

*This is a very moist bar and keeps well. May also be served warm with ice cream.*

| | | |
|---|---|---|
| **Large eggs** | **2** | **2** |
| **Granulated sugar** | **1 1/2 cups** | **375 mL** |
| **Can of fruit cocktail, with juice** | **14 oz.** | **398 mL** |
| **All-purpose flour** | **2 1/4 cups** | **550 mL** |
| **Baking soda** | **2 tsp.** | **10 mL** |
| **Vanilla extract** | **1 tsp.** | **5 mL** |
| **Salt** | **1/2 tsp.** | **2 mL** |
| | | |
| **Brown sugar, packed** | **1/2 cup** | **125 mL** |
| **Chopped walnuts** | **1/2 cup** | **125 mL** |
| | | |
| **WALNUT GLAZE** | | |
| **Brown sugar, packed** | **3/4 cup** | **175 mL** |
| **Butter (or hard margarine)** | **1/2 cup** | **125 mL** |
| **Chopped walnuts** | **1/2 cup** | **125 mL** |
| **Milk** | **1/4 cup** | **60 mL** |
| **Vanilla extract** | **1/2 tsp.** | **2 mL** |

Beat eggs and sugar in large bowl. Add fruit cocktail. Stir. Add next 4 ingredients. Stir well. Spread evenly in greased 9 x 13 inch (22 x 33 cm) pan.

Sprinkle brown sugar and walnuts over top. Bake in 350°F (175°C) oven for about 35 minutes until wooden pick inserted in centre comes out clean.

**Walnut Glaze:** Heat and stir all 5 ingredients in small, heavy saucepan on medium until mixture comes to a boil. Pour over warm fruit cocktail layer. Let stand in pan on wire rack until cool. Cuts into 54 squares.

*__1 square:__ 96 Calories; 3.3 g Total Fat (0.6 g Mono, 1.1 g Poly, 1.3 g Sat); 12 mg Cholesterol; 16 g Carbohydrate; trace Fibre; 1 g Protein; 86 mg Sodium*

Pictured on page 89.

# Cherry Almond Squares

*This is a rich, crumbly, melt-in-your-mouth square.*

| | | |
|---|---|---|
| All-purpose flour | 2 cups | 500 mL |
| Brown sugar, packed | 1 cup | 250 mL |
| Butter, softened | 1 cup | 250 mL |
| Finely chopped red glazed cherries | 1/2 cup | 125 mL |
| Chopped blanched almonds | 1/2 cup | 125 mL |
| **CHERRY ICING** | | |
| Icing (confectioner's) sugar | 1 1/2 cups | 375 mL |
| Butter (or hard margarine), softened | 3 tbsp. | 50 mL |
| Water | 1 1/2 tbsp. | 25 mL |
| Cherry extract | 1/2 tsp. | 2 mL |

Mix first 3 ingredients in large bowl until crumbly. Roll into ball with hands, ensuring no dry flour remains. Flatten slightly. Sprinkle cherries and almonds over dough. Press down lightly. Knead for 1 to 2 minutes, until well combined. Press firmly into ungreased 9 x 9 inch (22 x 22 cm) pan. Prick entire surface of dough with fork through to bottom of pan. Bake in 325°F (160°C) oven for about 25 minutes until just starting to turn golden. Let stand in pan on wire rack until cool.

**Cherry Icing:** Beat all 4 ingredients in small bowl until smooth, adding more water or icing sugar as necessary until spreading consistency. Spread evenly over bottom layer. Cuts into 36 squares.

*__1 square:__ 134 Calories; 6.8 g Total Fat (2.0 g Mono, 0.4 g Poly, 3.9 g Sat); 16 mg Cholesterol; 18 g Carbohydrate; trace Fibre; 1 g Protein; 47 mg Sodium*

Pictured on page 89.

# Chip Crumbles

*This is very quick and easy to make, and will remind you of chocolate chip cookies.*

| | | |
|---|---|---|
| All-purpose flour | 2 cups | 500 mL |
| Brown sugar, packed | 1 cup | 250 mL |
| Butter (or hard margarine), softened | 1 cup | 250 mL |
| Vanilla extract | 1 tsp. | 5 mL |
| Finely chopped walnuts | 1 cup | 250 mL |
| Semi-sweet chocolate chips | 1 cup | 250 mL |

*(continued on next page)*

Mix first 4 ingredients in large bowl until crumbly.

Add walnuts and chocolate chips. Stir. Press firmly into ungreased 9 x 9 inch (22 x 22 cm) pan. Bake in 350°F (175°C) oven for about 25 minutes until browned. Cool slightly. Cut while still warm into 36 squares.

*__1 square:__ 134 Calories; 8.6 g Total Fat (2.1 g Mono, 1.8 g Poly, 4.2 g Sat); 13 mg Cholesterol; 14 g Carbohydrate; 1 g Fibre; 1 g Protein; 39 mg Sodium*

Pictured on page 89.

# Neapolitan Squares

*An attractive colour contrast makes these squares as appealing to the eye as they are to the palate.*

| | | |
|---|---|---|
| **BOTTOM LAYER** | | |
| **Butter (or hard margarine)** | **1/2 cup** | **125 mL** |
| **Graham cracker crumbs** | **1 1/4 cups** | **300 mL** |
| **Brown sugar, packed** | **1/2 cup** | **125 mL** |
| **All-purpose flour** | **1/3 cup** | **75 mL** |
| **FILLING** | | |
| **Medium unsweetened coconut** | **2 cups** | **500 mL** |
| **Can of sweetened condensed milk** | **11 oz.** | **300 mL** |
| **ICING** | | |
| **Icing (confectioner's) sugar** | **2 cups** | **500 mL** |
| **Butter (or hard margarine), softened** | **1/4 cup** | **60 mL** |
| **Maraschino cherry juice (see Note)** | **3 tbsp.** | **50 mL** |

**Bottom Layer:** Melt butter in medium saucepan on medium. Remove from heat. Stir in next 3 ingredients. Press firmly into ungreased 9 x 9 inch (22 x 22 cm) pan. Bake in 350°F (175°C) oven for 10 minutes.

**Filling:** Combine coconut and condensed milk in medium bowl. Immediately spread evenly over bottom layer. Bake for about 20 minutes until edges start to turn golden. Let stand in pan on wire rack until cool.

**Icing:** Beat all 3 ingredients in medium bowl until smooth, adding more cherry juice or icing sugar as necessary until spreading consistency. Spread evenly over filling. Cover tightly. Let stand for at least 6 hours or overnight. Cuts into 36 squares.

*__1 square:__ 144 Calories; 7.4 g Total Fat (1.2 g Mono, 0.3 g Poly, 5 g Sat); 12 mg Cholesterol; 19 g Carbohydrate; 1 g Fibre; 1 g Protein; 58 mg Sodium*

Pictured on page 89.

**Note:** If you don't have any maraschino cherry juice, use water tinted with red food colouring and add 1/4 tsp. (1 mL) cherry or almond extract instead.

# Chocolate Walnut Slice

*A buttery fudge taste.*

| | | |
|---|---|---|
| **BOTTOM LAYER** | | |
| All-purpose flour | 1 1/4 cups | 300 mL |
| Butter (or hard margarine), softened | 1/2 cup | 125 mL |
| Brown sugar, packed | 1/3 cup | 75 mL |
| Salt | 1/4 tsp. | 1 mL |
| **MIDDLE LAYER** | | |
| Large eggs | 2 | 2 |
| Brown sugar, packed | 1 cup | 250 mL |
| Medium unsweetened coconut | 1 cup | 250 mL |
| Chopped walnuts | 1/2 cup | 125 mL |
| Cocoa, sifted if lumpy | 3 tbsp. | 50 mL |
| All-purpose flour | 1 tbsp. | 15 mL |
| Vanilla extract | 1 tsp. | 5 mL |
| **ICING** | | |
| Icing (confectioner's) sugar | 1 1/4 cups | 300 mL |
| Cocoa, sifted if lumpy | 1/3 cup | 75 mL |
| Butter (or hard margarine), softened | 3 tbsp. | 50 mL |
| Hot strong prepared coffee | 1 1/2 tbsp. | 25 mL |

**Bottom Layer:** Mix all 4 ingredients in medium bowl until crumbly. Press firmly into ungreased 9 x 9 inch (22 x 22 cm) pan. Set aside.

**Middle Layer:** Beat eggs and brown sugar in medium bowl until frothy. Add remaining 5 ingredients. Stir well. Spread evenly over bottom layer. Bake in 350°F (175°C) oven for 30 minutes. Let stand in pan on wire rack until cool.

**Icing:** Beat all 4 ingredients in small bowl until smooth, adding more coffee or icing sugar as necessary until spreading consistency. Spread evenly over middle layer. Cuts into 36 squares.

***1 square:** 126 Calories; 6.3 g Total Fat (1.1 g Mono, 0.9 g Poly, 3.6 g Sat); 21 mg Cholesterol; 17 g Carbohydrate; 1 g Fibre; 1 g Protein; 48 mg Sodium*

Pictured on page 89.

# Coconut Graham Cake

*This one-step cake is a sweet treat with or without the icing.*

| | | |
|---|---|---|
| Large eggs | 2 | 2 |
| Granulated sugar | 1 cup | 250 mL |
| Butter (or hard margarine), softened | 1/2 cup | 125 mL |
| Vanilla extract | 1 tsp. | 5 mL |
| Graham cracker crumbs | 2 cups | 450 mL |
| Medium unsweetened coconut | 1 cup | 250 mL |
| All-purpose flour | 3 tbsp. | 50 mL |
| Baking powder | 1 tsp. | 5 mL |
| Salt | 1/4 tsp. | 1 mL |
| ICING | | |
| Butter (or hard margarine) | 1/4 cup | 60 mL |
| Brown sugar, packed | 1/2 cup | 125 mL |
| Milk | 2 tbsp. | 30 mL |
| Icing (confectioner's) sugar | 1 cup | 250 mL |

Beat first 4 ingredients in large bowl until smooth.

Add next 5 ingredients. Stir well. Press firmly into greased 9 x 9 inch (22 x 22 cm) pan. Bake in 350°F (175°C) oven for about 25 minutes until wooden pick inserted in centre comes out clean. Let stand in pan on wire rack until cool.

**Icing:** Combine first 3 ingredients in small saucepan. Heat and stir on medium until melted. Bring to a boil. Reduce heat to medium-low. Simmer, uncovered, for 2 minutes, stirring occasionally. Transfer to medium bowl. Cool for about 30 minutes until lukewarm.

Add icing sugar. Beat until light and creamy, adding more milk or icing sugar as necessary until spreading consistency. Spread evenly over cake. Cuts into 36 squares.

***1 square:*** *120 Calories; 5.9 g Total Fat (1.2 g Mono, 0.3 g Poly, 3.7 g Sat); 22 mg Cholesterol; 17 g Carbohydrate; trace Fibre; 1 g Protein; 93 mg Sodium*

Pictured on page 89.

## *Paré Pointer*

*The most perfect shape in the world is round. Have another sweet.*

# Chocolate Date Nut Squares

*This is really an outstanding chocolate square—nice and moist.*

| | | |
|---|---|---|
| **Chopped pitted dates** | **1 cup** | **250 mL** |
| **Baking soda** | **1 tsp.** | **5 mL** |
| **Boiling water** | **1 1/2 cups** | **375 mL** |
| **Large eggs** | **2** | **2** |
| **Granulated sugar** | **1 cup** | **250 mL** |
| **Butter (or hard margarine), softened** | **1/2 cup** | **125 mL** |
| **All-purpose flour** | **1 1/2 cups** | **375 mL** |
| **Salt** | **3/4 tsp.** | **4 mL** |
| **Baking soda** | **3/4 tsp.** | **4 mL** |
| **CHOCOLATE NUT TOPPING** | | |
| **Semi-sweet chocolate chips** | **1 cup** | **250 mL** |
| **Brown sugar, packed** | **1/2 cup** | **125 mL** |
| **Chopped walnuts** | **1/2 cup** | **125 mL** |

Put dates into large, heatproof bowl. Sprinkle with first amount of baking soda. Pour boiling water over top. Stir. Let stand for about 5 minutes, until dates are softened.

Beat sugar and butter in medium bowl. Add eggs. Beat well. Add to date mixture. Combine next 3 ingredients in small bowl. Add to date mixture. Stir well. Batter will be thin. Spread evenly in greased 9 x 13 inch (22 x 33 cm) pan.

**Chocolate Nut Topping:** Combine all 3 ingredients in medium bowl. Sprinkle over batter in pan. Bake in 350°F (175°C) oven for about 50 minutes until wooden pick inserted in centre comes out clean. Let stand in pan on wire rack until cool. Cuts into 54 squares.

***1 square:*** *82 Calories; 3.5 g Total Fat (0.9 g Mono, 0.6 g Poly, 1.7 g Sat); 12 mg Cholesterol; 13 g Carbohydrate; 1 g Fibre; 1 g Protein; 89 mg Sodium*

Pictured on page 90.

1. Apricot Zings, page 75
2. Fruit Cocktail Bars, page 83
3. Quick Hurry Bars, page 81
4. Chocolate Walnut Slice, page 86
5. Chip Crumbles, page 84
6. Graham Cracker Chew, page 73
7. Cherry Triangles, page 78
8. Cherry Almond Squares, page 84
9. Neapolitan Squares, page 85
10. Coconut Graham Cake, page 87
11. Five Cup Slice, page 81

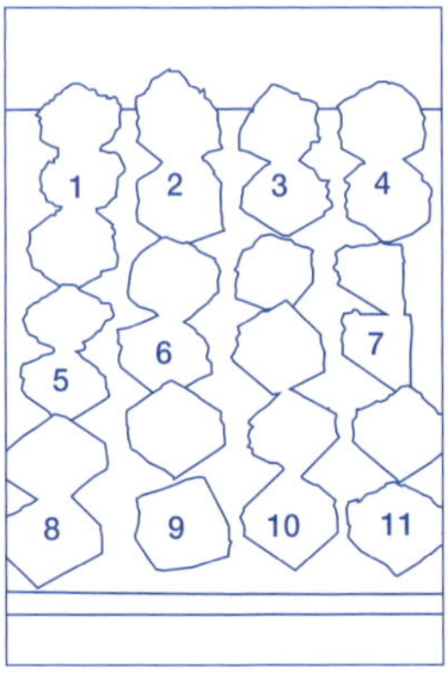

# Raspberry Bars

*Shredded coconut gives this a fancy and festive appearance.*

| | | |
|---|---|---|
| **BOTTOM LAYER** | | |
| **All-purpose flour** | **1 1/4 cups** | **300 mL** |
| **Butter (or hard margarine), softened** | **1/2 cup** | **125 mL** |
| **Granulated sugar** | **1/4 cup** | **60 mL** |
| **FILLING** | | |
| **Raspberry jam** | **1 cup** | **250 mL** |
| **COCONUT LAYER** | | |
| **Large eggs** | **2** | **2** |
| **Shredded coconut** | **2 cups** | **500 mL** |
| **Granulated sugar** | **1 cup** | **250 mL** |
| **All-purpose flour** | **1 tbsp.** | **15 mL** |
| **Vanilla extract** | **1 tsp.** | **5 mL** |
| **Baking powder** | **1/2 tsp.** | **2 mL** |

**Bottom Layer:** Mix all 3 ingredients in small bowl until crumbly. Press firmly into ungreased 9 x 9 inch (22 x 22 cm) pan. Bake in 350°F (175°C) oven for 15 minutes.

**Filling:** Drop rounded teaspoonfuls of jam over bottom layer. Spread evenly.

**Coconut Layer:** Beat eggs in large bowl until frothy. Add remaining 5 ingredients. Stir well. Spread evenly over filling. Bake for about 30 minutes until golden brown. Let stand in pan on wire rack until cool. Cuts into 36 squares.

***1 square:** 118 Calories; 5.4 g Total Fat (0.8 g Mono, 0.1 g Poly, 4.0 g Sat); 19 mg Cholesterol; 17 g Carbohydrate; 1 g Fibre; 1 g Protein; 31 mg Sodium*

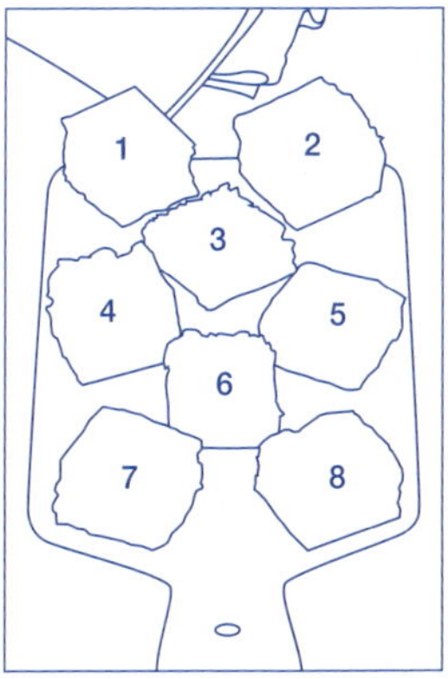


Pictured at left.

1. Molasses Bars, page 99
2. Chocolate Date Nut Squares, page 88
3. Raspberry Bars, above
4. Date Pecan Bars, page 95
5. Chocolate Orange Drops, page 101
6. Almond Date Squares, page 94
7. Cherry Squares, page 92
8. Merry Fruit Bars, page 96

# Cherry Squares

*This is one of the most popular squares. After you've tried it you'll understand why.*

| | | |
|---|---|---|
| BOTTOM LAYER | | |
| All-purpose flour | 1 1/4 cups | 300 mL |
| Butter (or hard margarine), softened | 1/2 cup | 125 mL |
| Brown sugar, packed | 1/3 cup | 75 mL |
| MIDDLE LAYER | | |
| Large eggs | 2 | 2 |
| Brown sugar, packed | 1 1/4 cups | 300 mL |
| Medium unsweetened coconut | 1 cup | 250 mL |
| Chopped walnuts | 1/2 cup | 125 mL |
| Red glazed (or maraschino) cherries, chopped | 1/2 cup | 125 mL |
| All-purpose flour | 1 tbsp. | 15 mL |
| Baking powder | 1/2 tsp. | 2 mL |
| Salt | 1/8 tsp. | 0.5 mL |
| ICING | | |
| Icing (confectioner's) sugar | 1 cup | 250 mL |
| Butter (or hard margarine), softened | 2 tbsp. | 30 mL |
| Milk | 1 tbsp. | 15 mL |
| Vanilla extract | 1/2 tsp. | 2 mL |

**Bottom Layer:** Mix all 3 ingredients in small bowl until crumbly. Press firmly into ungreased 9 x 9 inch (22 x 22 cm) pan. Bake in 350°F (175°C) oven for 15 minutes.

**Middle Layer:** Beat eggs in medium bowl until frothy. Add remaining 7 ingredients. Mix well. Spread evenly over bottom layer. Bake for about 25 minutes until golden. Let stand in pan on wire rack until cool.

**Icing:** Beat all 4 ingredients in small bowl until smooth, adding more milk or icing sugar as necessary until spreading consistency. Spread evenly over middle layer. Cuts into 36 squares.

*__1 square:__ 129 Calories; 5.8 g Total Fat (1.0 g Mono, 0.9 g Poly, 3.4 g Sat); 20 mg Cholesterol; 19 g Carbohydrate; 1 g Fibre; 1 g Protein; 49 mg Sodium*

Pictured on page 90.

# Chocolate Fruit Squares

*A fruity bar with three appealing layers of chocolate, cherries and vanilla icing.*

| | | |
|---|---|---|
| **BOTTOM LAYER** | | |
| **All-purpose flour** | **1 cup** | **250 mL** |
| **Butter (or hard margarine), softened** | **1/2 cup** | **125 mL** |
| **Cocoa, sifted if lumpy** | **1/4 cup** | **60 mL** |
| **Granulated sugar** | **1/4 cup** | **60 mL** |
| **MIDDLE LAYER** | | |
| **Large eggs** | **2** | **2** |
| **Brown sugar, packed** | **1/2 cup** | **125 mL** |
| **Finely chopped pitted dates** | **3/4 cup** | **175 mL** |
| **Finely chopped red glazed cherries** | **3/4 cup** | **175 mL** |
| **All-purpose flour** | **1 tbsp.** | **15 mL** |
| **Lemon juice** | **1 tsp.** | **5 mL** |
| **Vanilla extract** | **1/2 tsp.** | **2 mL** |
| **ICING** | | |
| **Icing (confectioner's) sugar** | **1 1/2 cups** | **375 mL** |
| **Butter (or hard margarine), softened** | **3 tbsp.** | **50 mL** |
| **Vanilla extract** | **1/2 tsp.** | **2 mL** |
| **Milk (or water)** | **1 1/2 tbsp.** | **25 mL** |

**Bottom Layer:** Mix all 4 ingredients in medium bowl until crumbly. Press firmly into ungreased 9 x 9 inch (22 x 22 cm) pan. Bake in 350°F (175°C) oven for 10 minutes.

**Middle Layer:** Beat eggs and brown sugar in medium bowl. Add next 5 ingredients. Mix well. Spread evenly over bottom layer. Bake for about 25 minutes until set and golden brown. Let stand in pan on wire rack until cool.

**Icing:** Beat all 4 ingredients in small bowl for 1 minute until spreading consistency, adding more icing sugar or milk if needed. Spread evenly over middle layer. Cuts into 36 squares.

***1 square:*** *108 Calories; 3.8 g Total Fat (0.9 g Mono, 0.1 g Poly, 2.3 g Sat); 21 mg Cholesterol; 18 g Carbohydrate; trace Fibre; 1 g Protein; 33 mg Sodium*

Pictured on page 107.

# Almond Date Squares

*Truly a delicious treat. Cover to store, so the meringue has a chance to soften.*

| | | |
|---|---|---|
| **BOTTOM LAYER** | | |
| Egg yolks (large) | 2 | 2 |
| All-purpose flour | 1 1/2 cups | 375 mL |
| Butter (or hard margarine), softened | 1/2 cup | 125 mL |
| Granulated sugar | 1/2 cup | 125 mL |
| Baking powder | 1 tsp. | 5 mL |
| Vanilla extract | 1 tsp. | 5 mL |
| **FILLING** | | |
| Chopped pitted dates | 1 cup | 250 mL |
| Water | 1/2 cup | 125 mL |
| **TOP LAYER** | | |
| Egg whites (large), room temperature | 2 | 2 |
| Brown sugar, packed | 1 cup | 250 mL |
| Sliced (or slivered) almonds | 3 tbsp. | 50 mL |

**Bottom Layer:** Mix all 6 ingredients until crumbly. Press firmly into greased 9 x 9 inch (22 x 22 cm) pan. Set aside.

**Filling:** Combine dates and water in small saucepan. Bring to a boil. Reduce heat to medium-low. Simmer, uncovered, for 5 to 10 minutes, until dates are softened and water is almost evaporated. Add more water while simmering if necessary to soften dates. Transfer to small bowl. Cool slightly. Spread evenly over bottom layer.

**Top Layer:** Beat egg whites in medium bowl until frothy. Slowly add brown sugar, 1/3 cup (75 mL) at a time, beating after each addition until stiff peaks form. Spoon over filling. Spread evenly.

Sprinkle with almonds. Bake in 350°F (175°C) oven for 30 minutes. Let stand in pan on wire rack until cool. Cuts into 36 squares.

***1 square:** 94 Calories; 3.1 g Total Fat (0.9 g Mono, 0.2 g Poly, 1.7 g Sat); 18 mg Cholesterol; 16 g Carbohydrate; trace Fibre; 1 g Protein; 39 mg Sodium*

Pictured on page 90.

### *Paré Pointer*

*While at a church potluck supper, eat lots. Food for the soul has no calories.*

# Date Pecan Bars

*A picture won't tell the tale of these squares—it takes a taste to appreciate the rum flavour inside. Must be made a day or two ahead so the flavours can mellow.*

| | | |
|---|---|---|
| **Chopped pitted dates** | **1 cup** | **250 mL** |
| **Butter (or hard margarine)** | **1/2 cup** | **125 mL** |
| **Baking soda** | **1 tsp.** | **5 mL** |
| **Boiling water** | **3/4 cup** | **175 mL** |
| **Dark (navy) rum (or 2 tsp., 10 mL, rum extract plus 1/4 cup, 60 mL, water)** | **1/4 cup** | **60 mL** |
| **Large egg** | **1** | **1** |
| **Granulated sugar** | **1/2 cup** | **125 mL** |
| **Vanilla extract** | **1 tsp.** | **5 mL** |
| **All-purpose flour** | **1 1/2 cups** | **375 mL** |
| **Baking powder** | **1 tsp.** | **5 mL** |
| **TOPPING** | | |
| **Brown sugar, packed** | **1 cup** | **250 mL** |
| **Butter (or hard margarine), softened** | **3 tbsp.** | **50 mL** |
| **Chopped pecans** | **1 cup** | **250 mL** |
| **Half-and-half cream** | **3 tbsp.** | **50 mL** |

Put dates and butter into large heatproof bowl. Sprinkle with baking soda. Pour boiling water over top. Stir until butter is melted. Add rum. Stir. Let stand for about 5 minutes, until dates are softened.

Beat next 3 ingredients in small bowl until combined. Add to date mixture. Add flour and baking powder. Stir well. Spread evenly in greased 9 x 9 inch (22 x 22 cm) pan. Bake in 350°F (175°C) oven for 25 minutes.

**Topping:** Mix brown sugar and butter in small bowl until crumbly. Add pecans and cream. Mix well. Immediately spread evenly over date layer. Bake for 15 to 20 minutes until golden. Let stand in pan on wire rack until cool. Cover tightly. Let stand for at least 6 hours or overnight. Cuts into 36 squares.

***1 square:** 126 Calories; 6.1 g Total Fat (2.3 g Mono, 0.9 g Poly, 2.5 g Sat); 16 mg Cholesterol; 17 g Carbohydrate; 1 g Fibre; 1 g Protein; 80 mg Sodium*

Pictured on page 90.

# Merry Fruit Bars

*This fruity bar goes great with tea.*

| | | |
|---|---|---|
| Large eggs | 2 | 2 |
| Granulated sugar | 1/2 cup | 125 mL |
| Vanilla extract | 1/2 tsp. | 2 mL |
| All-purpose flour | 3/4 cup | 175 mL |
| Chopped mixed glazed fruit | 3/4 cup | 175 mL |
| Chopped walnuts | 1/2 cup | 125 mL |
| Chopped pitted dates | 1/4 cup | 60 mL |
| Baking powder | 3/4 tsp. | 4 mL |
| Salt | 1/2 tsp. | 2 mL |

Beat eggs in medium bowl until thickened and increased in volume. Add sugar and vanilla. Beat well.

Add remaining 6 ingredients. Stir well. Spread in greased 8 x 8 inch (20 x 20 cm) pan. Bake in 350°F (175°C) oven for about 30 minutes until set. Let stand in pan on wire rack until cool. Cuts into 25 squares.

***1 square:** 76 Calories; 1.9 g Total Fat (0.2 g Mono, 1.1 g Poly, 0.3 g Sat); 17 mg Cholesterol; 14 g Carbohydrate; trace Fibre; 1 g Protein; 75 mg Sodium*

Pictured on page 90.

# Australian Honey Bars

*An Australian woman gave me the recipe for this moist and chewy bar that's done in one step.*

| | | |
|---|---|---|
| Liquid honey | 1/2 cup | 125 mL |
| Butter (or hard margarine), softened | 6 tbsp. | 100 mL |
| Large eggs | 3 | 3 |
| All-purpose flour | 1 1/2 cups | 375 mL |
| Raisins (or currants) | 1 cup | 250 mL |
| Chopped walnuts | 3/4 cup | 175 mL |
| Baking powder | 1 tsp. | 5 mL |
| Icing (confectioner's) sugar, for dusting | | |

Beat honey and butter in large bowl. Add eggs 1 at a time, beating well after each addition.

*(continued on next page)*

Add next 4 ingredients. Stir until just combined. Spread evenly in greased 9 x 9 inch (22 x 22 cm) pan. Bake in 350°F (175°C) oven for about 30 minutes until firm. Let stand in pan on wire rack until cool.

Just before serving, dust with icing sugar. Cuts into 36 squares.

***1 square:*** *86 Calories; 3.9 g Total Fat (0.7 g Mono, 1.3 g Poly, 1.5 g Sat); 23 mg Cholesterol; 12 g Carbohydrate; trace Fibre; 2 g Protein; 35 mg Sodium*

Pictured on page 107.

# Prune Chips

*You'll never know how good prunes can taste until you try this.*

| | | |
|---|---|---|
| **Large egg** | **1** | **1** |
| **Butter (or hard margarine), softened** | **1/2 cup** | **125 mL** |
| **Granulated sugar** | **1 cup** | **250 mL** |
| **Water** | **1/2 cup** | **125 mL** |
| **Lemon juice** | **2 tsp.** | **10 mL** |
| **Finely chopped, pitted prunes** | **2/3 cup** | **150 mL** |
| **Chopped walnuts** | **1/3 cup** | **75 mL** |
| **All-purpose flour** | **1 1/2 cups** | **375 mL** |
| **Baking powder** | **1/2 tsp.** | **2 mL** |
| **Baking soda** | **1/2 tsp.** | **2 mL** |
| **Ground cinnamon** | **1/2 tsp.** | **2 mL** |
| **Ground nutmeg** | **1/2 tsp.** | **2 mL** |
| **Salt** | **1/2 tsp.** | **2 mL** |
| **Ground cloves** | **1/4 tsp.** | **1 mL** |

Beat first 3 ingredients in large bowl until smooth. Add water and lemon juice. Beat well.

Add prunes and walnuts. Stir.

Combine remaining 7 ingredients in medium bowl. Add to prune mixture. Stir until just combined. Spread evenly in greased 9 x 9 inch (22 x 22 cm) pan. Bake in 350°F (175°C) oven for about 45 minutes until wooden pick inserted in centre comes out clean. Let stand in pan on wire rack until cool. Cuts into 36 squares.

***1 square:*** *80 Calories; 3.4 g Total Fat (0.8 g Mono, 0.6 g Poly, 1.7 g Sat); 13 mg Cholesterol; 12 g Carbohydrate; trace Fibre; 1 g Protein; 77 mg Sodium*

Pictured on page 107.

# Raisin Squares

*For a not-too-sweet square, this is a good choice.*

| | | |
|---|---|---|
| **Baking soda** | **1 tsp.** | **5 mL** |
| **Raisins** | **1 cup** | **250 mL** |
| **Boiling water** | **1/2 cup** | **125 mL** |
| **Butter (or hard margarine), softened** | **1/2 cup** | **125 mL** |
| **Granulated sugar** | **2/3 cup** | **150 mL** |
| **Large egg** | **1** | **1** |
| **Vanilla extract** | **1 tsp.** | **5 mL** |
| **All-purpose flour** | **1 1/3 cups** | **325 mL** |
| **Baking powder** | **1 tsp.** | **5 mL** |
| **Salt** | **1/8 tsp.** | **0.5 mL** |

**Icing (confectioner's) sugar, for dusting**

Bring raisins and water to a boil in small saucepan. Remove from heat. Add baking soda. Stir. Cool.

Beat butter and sugar in medium bowl. Add egg and vanilla. Beat well. Add raisin mixture. Stir.

Combine next 3 ingredients in small bowl. Add to raisin mixture. Stir well. Spread evenly in greased 9 x 9 inch (22 x 22 cm) pan. Bake in 350°F (175°C) oven for 35 to 40 minutes until golden. Let stand in pan on wire rack until cool.

Just before serving, dust with icing sugar. Cuts into 36 squares.

***1 square:** 69 Calories; 2.7 g Total Fat (0.7 g Mono, 0.1 g Poly, 1.6 g Sat); 13 mg Cholesterol; 11 g Carbohydrate; trace Fibre; 1 g Protein; 79 mg Sodium*

Pictured on page 107.

# Condensed Squares

*Sweetened condensed milk also condenses the time this square needs in the oven.*

| | | |
|---|---|---|
| **Flaked coconut** | **1 1/2 cups** | **375 mL** |
| **Graham cracker crumbs** | **1 1/2 cups** | **375 mL** |
| **Can of sweetened condensed milk** | **11 oz.** | **300 mL** |
| **Chopped walnuts** | **1 cup** | **250 mL** |
| **Cocoa, sifted if lumpy** | **1/3 cup** | **75 mL** |
| **Vanilla extract** | **1 tsp.** | **5 mL** |

*(continued on next page)*

Combine all 6 ingredients in large bowl. Press firmly into greased 8 x 8 inch (20 x 20 cm) pan. Bake in 350°F (175°C) oven for 30 to 35 minutes until golden. Let stand in pan on wire rack until cool. Cuts into 25 squares.

***1 square:*** *120 Calories; 6.2 g Total Fat (0.8 g Mono, 2.5 g Poly, 2.3 g Sat); 3.3 mg Cholesterol; 15 g Carbohydrate; 1 g Fibre; 2 g Protein; 57 mg Sodium*

Pictured on page 107.

# Molasses Bars

*Add this to your list of squares that aren't too sweet.*

| | | |
|---|---|---|
| **Butter (or hard margarine), softened** | **1/2 cup** | **125 mL** |
| **Granulated sugar** | **1/2 cup** | **125 mL** |
| **Large egg, fork-beaten** | **1** | **1** |
| **Fancy (mild) molasses** | **1/4 cup** | **60 mL** |
| **Ground cinnamon** | **1/2 tsp.** | **2 mL** |
| **Ground cloves** | **1/4 tsp.** | **1 mL** |
| **Ground ginger** | **1/4 tsp.** | **1 mL** |
| **Salt** | **1/4 tsp.** | **1 mL** |
| **Hot strong prepared coffee** | **1/2 cup** | **125 mL** |
| **All-purpose flour** | **1 1/4 cups** | **300 mL** |
| **Baking soda** | **1/2 tsp.** | **2 mL** |
| **ICING** | | |
| **Icing (confectioner's) sugar)** | **1 1/2 cups** | **375 mL** |
| **Butter (or hard margarine), softened** | **3 tbsp.** | **50 mL** |
| **Orange juice** | **1 1/2 tbsp.** | **25 mL** |

Beat butter and sugar in large bowl. Add next 6 ingredients. Beat well. Add 1/4 cup (60 mL) coffee. Stir.

Combine flour and baking soda in small bowl. Add to molasses mixture in 2 additions, alternating with remaining 1/4 cup (60 mL) coffee in 1 addition, stirring well after each addition. Spread evenly in greased 9 x 9 inch (22 x 22 cm) pan. Bake in 350°F (175°C) oven for 20 to 25 minutes until wooden pick inserted in centre comes out clean. Let stand in pan on wire rack until cool.

**Icing:** Beat all 3 ingredients in small bowl until smooth, adding more orange juice or icing sugar as necessary until spreading consistency. Spread evenly over bottom layer. Cuts into 36 squares.

***1 square:*** *84 Calories; 3.6 g Total Fat (0.9 g Mono, 0.1 g Poly, 2.2 g Sat); 15 mg Cholesterol; 13 g Carbohydrate; trace Fibre; 1 g Protein; 61 mg Sodium*

Pictured on page 90.

# Tweed Squares

*A distinguished square with a smooth finish.*

| | | |
|---|---|---|
| **BOTTOM LAYER** | | |
| Egg whites (large), room temperature | 2 | 2 |
| Butter (or hard margarine), softened | 1/2 cup | 125 mL |
| Granulated sugar | 2/3 cup | 150 mL |
| All-purpose flour | 1 1/3 cups | 325 mL |
| Baking powder | 2 tsp. | 10 mL |
| Salt | 1/2 tsp. | 2 mL |
| Milk | 1/2 cup | 125 mL |
| Semi-sweet chocolate baking squares (1oz., 28 g, each), finely grated | 2 | 2 |
| **VANILLA ICING** | | |
| Icing (confectioner's) sugar | 1 1/2 cups | 375 mL |
| Butter (or hard margarine), softened | 3 tbsp. | 50 mL |
| Water | 1 1/2 tbsp. | 25 mL |
| Vanilla extract | 1/2 tsp. | 2 mL |
| **TOPPING** | | |
| Semi-sweet chocolate baking squares (1 oz., 28 g), chopped | 2 | 2 |
| Butter (or hard margarine) | 1 tbsp. | 15 mL |

**Bottom Layer:** Beat egg whites in separate small bowl until stiff peaks form. Set aside. Beat butter and sugar with same beaters in large bowl.

Combine next 3 ingredients in small bowl. Add to butter mixture in 2 additions, alternating with milk in 1 addition, stirring well after each addition. Fold reserved egg whites into batter until no white streaks remain.

Fold in grated chocolate. Spread evenly in greased 9 x 9 inch (22 x 22 cm) pan. Bake in 350°F (175°C) oven for about 35 minutes until golden. Let stand in pan on wire rack until cool.

**Vanilla Icing:** Beat all 4 ingredients in small bowl until smooth, adding more water or icing sugar as necessary until spreading consistency. Spread evenly over bottom layer. Let stand for about 1 hour until set.

*(continued on next page)*

**Topping:** Heat chocolate and butter in small, heavy saucepan on lowest heat, stirring often, until chocolate is almost melted. Remove from heat. Stir until smooth. Cool slightly. Spread evenly over icing. Chill until set. Cuts into 36 squares.

*__1 square:__ 99 Calories; 4.3 g Total Fat (1.2 g Mono, 0.2 g Poly, 2.7 g Sat); 10 mg Cholesterol; 15 g Carbohydrate; trace Fibre; 1 g Protein; 95 mg Sodium*

Pictured on page 107.

# Chocolate Orange Drops

*Orange and chocolate go great together, and are a popular treat at Christmas time. Allow to cool to room temperature before serving.*

| | | |
|---|---|---|
| **Butter (or hard margarine), softened** | **1/2 cup** | **125 mL** |
| **Cream cheese, softened** | **4 oz.** | **125 g** |
| **Large egg** | **1** | **1** |
| **Icing (confectioner's) sugar** | **1/2 cup** | **125 mL** |
| **Grated orange zest** | **1 tbsp.** | **15 mL** |
| **Vanilla extract** | **1 tsp.** | **5 mL** |
| **All-purpose flour** | **1 cup** | **250 mL** |
| **Semi-sweet chocolate chips** | **1 cup** | **250 mL** |
| **Salt** | **1/2 tsp.** | **2 mL** |
| **ICING** | | |
| **Cream cheese, softened** | **4 oz.** | **125 g** |
| **Frozen concentrated orange juice, thawed** | **3 tbsp.** | **50 mL** |
| **Icing (confectioner's) sugar** | **1 1/2 cups** | **375 mL** |

Beat butter and cream cheese until light and fluffy. Add egg and icing sugar. Beat until smooth. Add orange zest and vanilla. Stir.

Combine next 3 ingredients in small bowl. Add to cream cheese mixture. Stir. Spread evenly in greased 9 x 9 inch (22 x 22 cm) pan. Bake in 350°F (175°C) oven for 25 to 30 minutes until set. Let stand in pan on wire rack until cool.

**Icing:** Beat next 3 ingredients in small bowl until smooth, adding more orange juice or icing sugar as necessary until spreading consistency. Spread evenly over cream cheese layer. Cuts into 36 squares.

*__1 square:__ 107 Calories; 6.2 g Total Fat (1.1 g Mono, 0.1 g Poly, 3.9 g Sat); 19 mg Cholesterol; 13 g Carbohydrate; trace Fibre; 1 g Protein; 74 mg Sodium*

Pictured on page 90.

# Marmalade Bars

*A tasty bar with great orange flavour.*

| | | |
|---|---|---|
| Large egg, fork-beaten | 1 | 1 |
| All-purpose flour | 2 cups | 500 mL |
| Brown sugar, packed | 3/4 cup | 175 mL |
| Butter (or hard margarine), softened | 3/4 cup | 175 mL |
| Grated orange zest | 1/4 cup | 60 mL |
| Salt | 1/8 tsp. | 0.5 mL |
| Orange marmalade | 1 cup | 250 mL |
| ICING | | |
| Icing (confectioner's) sugar | 1 1/2 cups | 375 mL |
| Butter (or hard margarine), softened | 3 tbsp. | 50 mL |
| Orange marmalade | 2 tbsp. | 30 mL |
| Orange extract | 1/4 tsp. | 1 mL |

Mix first 6 ingredients in large bowl until crumbly. Press 2/3 of flour mixture firmly into ungreased 9 x 9 inch (22 x 22 cm) pan. Reserve remaining flour mixture.

Drop rounded teaspoonfuls of marmalade over crumb mixture. Spread evenly. Sprinkle with reserved flour mixture. Press down gently. Bake in 350°F (175°C) oven for about 25 minutes until golden brown. Let stand in pan on wire rack until cool.

**Icing:** Beat all 4 ingredients in small bowl, adding more water or icing sugar as necessary until spreading consistency. Spread evenly over square. Cuts into 36 squares.

*__1 square:__ 128 Calories; 4.9 g Total Fat (1.3 g Mono, 0.2 g Poly, 3.0 g Sat); 18 mg Cholesterol; 21 g Carbohydrate; trace Fibre; 1 g Protein; 51 mg Sodium*

Pictured on page 107.

# Potato Chip Bars

*Potato chips make this a favourite for kids.*

| | | |
|---|---|---|
| Butter (or hard margarine), softened | 1 cup | 250 mL |
| Granulated sugar | 1/2 cup | 125 mL |
| Vanilla extract | 1 tsp. | 5 mL |
| All-purpose flour | 2 cups | 500 mL |

*(continued on next page)*

| | | |
|---|---|---|
| **Crushed potato chips** | **1 cup** | **250 mL** |
| **Finely chopped walnuts** | **1/2 cup** | **125 mL** |

Mix first 4 ingredients in large bowl until crumbly. Roll into ball with hands, ensuring no dry flour remains. Flatten slightly.

Sprinkle potato chips and walnuts over dough. Press down lightly. Knead for 1 to 2 minutes, until well combined. Press firmly into ungreased 9 x 9 inch (22 x 22 cm) pan. Bake in 350°F (175°C) oven for 15 to 20 minutes until set. Cool slightly. Cut while still warm into 36 squares.

***1 square:*** *100 Calories; 6.6 g Total Fat (1.5 g Mono, 1.0 g Poly, 3.3 g Sat); 13 mg Cholesterol; 10 g Carbohydrate; trace Fibre; 1 g Protein; 43 mg Sodium*

Pictured on page 108.

# Coconut Lemon Bars

*For both coconut and lemon flavour, this is a winner. Richer than other lemon bars.*

| | | |
|---|---|---|
| **BOTTOM LAYER** | | |
| **All-purpose flour** | **1 cup** | **250 mL** |
| **Brown sugar, packed** | **1/2 cup** | **125 mL** |
| **Butter (or hard margarine), softened** | **1/2 cup** | **125 mL** |
| **TOP LAYER** | | |
| **Large eggs** | **2** | **2** |
| **Brown sugar, packed** | **1 cup** | **250 mL** |
| **Chopped walnuts** | **1 cup** | **250 mL** |
| **Medium unsweetened coconut** | **1 cup** | **250 mL** |
| **Coarsely chopped raisins (or currants)** | **1/2 cup** | **125 mL** |
| **Lemon juice** | **2 tbsp.** | **30 mL** |
| **Grated lemon zest** | **1 tsp.** | **5 mL** |
| **Salt** | **1/4 tsp.** | **1 mL** |

**Bottom Layer:** Mix all 3 ingredients in medium bowl until crumbly. Press firmly into ungreased 9 x 9 inch (22 x 22 cm) pan. Bake in 350°F (175°C) oven for 10 minutes.

**Top Layer:** Beat eggs until frothy. Add remaining 7 ingredients. Stir well. Spread evenly over bottom layer. Bake for about 25 minutes until golden brown. Cool slightly. Cut while still warm into 36 squares.

***1 square:*** *110 Calories; 5.2 g Total Fat (1.0 g Mono, 1.7 g Poly, 2.0 g Sat); 19 mg Cholesterol; 15 g Carbohydrate; 1 g Fibre; 2 g Protein; 42 mg Sodium*

Pictured on page 107.

# Baked Fruit Roll

*And now for something completely different...bake the squares and then form into a log for slicing.*

| | | |
|---|---|---|
| **Large eggs** | **2** | **2** |
| **Granulated sugar** | **1 cup** | **250 mL** |
| **Chopped pitted dates** | **1 cup** | **250 mL** |
| **Chopped walnuts** | **1 cup** | **250 mL** |
| **Medium unsweetened coconut** | **1 cup** | **250 mL** |
| **Vanilla extract** | **1 tsp.** | **5 mL** |
| **Almond extract** | **1/4 tsp.** | **1 mL** |
| **Granulated sugar** | **2 tbsp.** | **30 mL** |

Beat eggs in medium bowl until frothy. Slowly add sugar, beating constantly, until thickened.

Add next 5 ingredients. Mix well. Press firmly into ungreased 2 quart (2 L) casserole. Bake uncovered in 350°F (175°C) oven for 30 minutes. Let stand on wire rack for 20 minutes. Stir, scraping down sides, until mixture is cool enough to handle. Shape into 9 inch (22 cm) long log, about 2 inches (5 cm) in diameter.

Sprinkle sugar evenly over sheet of waxed paper, slightly longer than log. Roll log in sugar until coated. Chill for at least 6 hours or overnight. Cut into 1/4 inch (6 mm) slices. Cuts into 36 slices.

***1 slice:** 46 Calories; 1.8 g Total Fat (0.3 g Mono, 1.2 g Poly, 0.2 g Sat); 8 mg Cholesterol; 7 g Carbohydrate; trace Fibre; 1 g Protein; 3 mg Sodium*

Pictured on page 108.

# Easy Graham Bars

ok *Sweetly simple to make.*

| | | |
|---|---|---|
| **Graham cracker crumbs** | **3 cups** | **750 mL** |
| **Chopped walnuts** | **1 cup** | **250 mL** |
| **Evaporated milk (or half-and-half cream)** | **1 cup** | **250 mL** |
| **Granulated sugar** | **1 cup** | **250 mL** |
| **Semi-sweet chocolate chips** | **1 cup** | **250 mL** |
| **Butter (or hard margarine), softened** | **1/4 cup** | **60 mL** |
| **Vanilla extract** | **1 tsp.** | **5 mL** |

*(continued on next page)*

Stir all 7 ingredients in large bowl until well combined. Spread evenly in greased 9 x 9 inch (22 x 22 cm) pan. Bake in 350°F (175°C) oven for about 35 minutes until set. Let stand in pan on wire rack until cool. Cuts into 36 bars.

***1 bar:*** *116 Calories; 6.0 g Total Fat (1.5 g Mono, 2.0 g Poly, 2.3 g Sat); 6 mg Cholesterol; 15 g Carbohydrate; 1 g Fibre; 2 g Protein; 59 mg Sodium*

Pictured on page 108.

# Orange Squares

*The sweet tang of oranges fills this entire square. You'll need a food processor for this one.*

| | | |
|---|---|---|
| **Medium unpeeled orange** | **1** | **1** |
| **Raisins (or currants)** | **1 cup** | **250 mL** |
| **Butter (or hard margarine), softened** | **1/2 cup** | **125 mL** |
| **Granulated sugar** | **1 cup** | **250 mL** |
| **Large egg** | **1** | **1** |
| **All-purpose flour** | **2 cups** | **500 mL** |
| **Baking powder** | **1/2 tsp.** | **2 mL** |
| **Salt** | **1/4 tsp.** | **1 mL** |
| **GLAZE** | | |
| **Reserved orange juice** | **2 tbsp.** | **30 mL** |
| **Icing (confectioner's) sugar** | **1 1/2 cups** | **375 mL** |

Cut orange into quarters. Squeeze 2 tbsp. (30 mL) juice into small cup. Set aside. Process orange pieces and raisins (or currants) in food processor until finely chopped.

Beat butter and sugar in large bowl. Add egg. Beat well.

Add next 3 ingredients and orange mixture. Mix well. Batter will be stiff. Press firmly into greased 9 x 13 inch (22 x 33 cm) pan. Bake in 350°F (175°C) oven for 25 minutes. Cool slightly.

**Glaze:** Beat reserved orange juice and icing sugar until smooth, adding more orange juice or icing sugar until barely pourable consistency. Spread evenly over top. Let stand until set. Cuts into 54 squares.

***1 square:*** *69 Calories; 1.8 g Total Fat (0.5 g Mono, 0.1 g Poly, 1.1 g Sat); 8 mg Cholesterol; 13 g Carbohydrate; trace Fibre; 1 g Protein; 30 mg Sodium*

Pictured on page 108.

# Pineapple Filled Bars

*The thick layer of pineapple gives these bars their unique flavour and helps to keep them moist.*

| | | |
|---|---|---|
| **BOTTOM LAYER** | | |
| Medium unsweetened coconut | 1 1/2 cups | 350 mL |
| All-purpose flour | 1 cup | 250 mL |
| Brown sugar, packed | 1 cup | 250 mL |
| Butter (or hard margarine), softened | 1/2 cup | 125 mL |
| Salt | 1/8 tsp. | 0.5 mL |
| **FILLING** | | |
| Crushed pineapple (with juice) | 1 cup | 250 mL |
| Granulated sugar | 3/4 cup | 175 mL |
| Cornstarch | 3 tbsp. | 50 mL |
| Butter (or hard margarine) | 1 tbsp. | 15 mL |
| Lemon juice | 1 tbsp. | 15 mL |

**Bottom Layer:** Mix all 5 ingredients in large bowl until crumbly. Spread 2/3 of coconut mixture evenly in greased 9 x 9 inch (22 x 22 cm) pan. Reserve remaining coconut mixture.

**Filling:** Combine all 5 ingredients in small saucepan. Bring to a boil on medium, stirring constantly. Remove from heat. Let stand for about 10 minutes, until cooled slightly. Spread evenly over bottom layer. Sprinkle with reserved coconut mixture. Press down gently. Bake in 350°F (175°C) oven for about 25 minutes until golden brown. Cool slightly. Cut while still warm into 36 squares.

***1 square:*** *102 Calories; 4.8 g Total Fat (0.8 g Mono, 0.1 g Poly, 3.6 g Sat); 8 mg Cholesterol; 15 g Carbohydrate; 1 g Fibre; 1 g Protein; 32 mg Sodium*

Pictured on page 108.

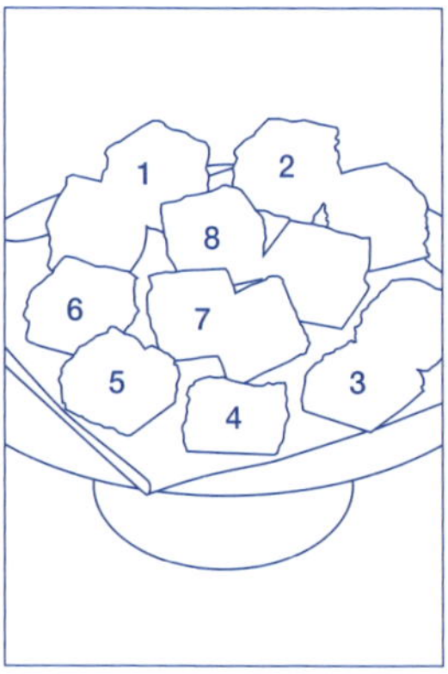


1. Prune Chips, page 97
2. Australian Honey Bars, page 96
3. Marmalade Bars, page 102
4. Coconut Lemon Bars, page 103
5. Condensed Squares, page 98
6. Raisin Squares, page 98
7. Chocolate Fruit Squares, page 93
8. Tweed Squares, page 100

Props courtesy of: Cherison Enterprises Inc.

# Chinese Chews

*Tradition has it that each "chew" be rolled in icing sugar, but you can sift the sugar over top to avoid handling each one individually.*

| | | |
|---|---|---|
| **Chopped pitted dates** | **1 cup** | **250 mL** |
| **Granulated sugar** | **1 cup** | **250 mL** |
| **All-purpose flour** | **3/4 cup** | **175 mL** |
| **Chopped walnuts** | **1/2 cup** | **125 mL** |
| **Baking powder** | **1 tsp.** | **5 mL** |
| **Salt** | **1/4 tsp.** | **1 mL** |
| **Large eggs** | **2** | **2** |
| **Icing (confectioner's) sugar, for dusting** | | |

Combine first 6 ingredients in large bowl.

Beat eggs in small bowl until smooth. Add to date mixture. Stir well. Spread evenly in greased 9 x 9 inch (22 x 22 cm) pan. Bake in 350°F (175°C) oven for about 25 minutes until wooden pick inserted in centre comes out clean. Let stand in pan on wire rack until cool.

Just before serving, dust with icing sugar. Cuts into 36 squares.

***1 square:** 59 Calories; 1.4 g Total Fat (0.3 g Mono, 0.8 g Poly, 0.2 g Sat); 12 mg Cholesterol; 11 g Carbohydrate; trace Fibre; 1 g Protein; 35 mg Sodium*

Pictured on page 125.

**Variation:** For a different presentation, cut into squares while still warm. Roll each square individually in icing sugar until coated.

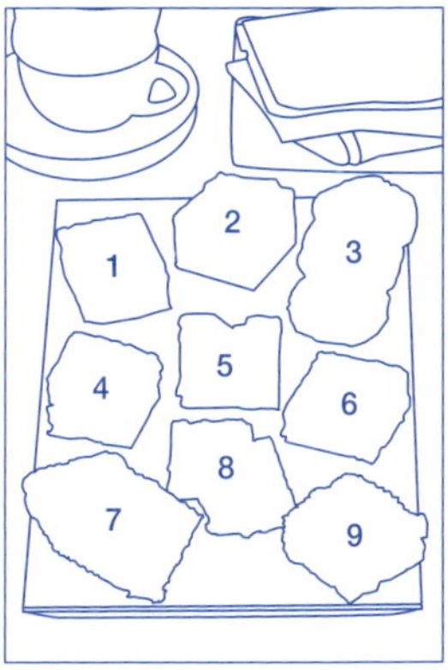


1. Nutted Gum Drops, page 113
2. Chewy Nut Bars, page 111
3. Baked Fruit Roll, page 104
4. Easy Graham Bars, page 104
5. Frieda's Number 89, page 110
6. Orange Squares, page 105
7. Pineapple Filled Bars, page 106
8. Potato Chip Bars, page 102
9. Three Layer Slice, page 112

Props courtesy of: Cherison Enterprises Inc.

# Frieda's Number 89

*A cranberry spice bar that tastes like your favourite apple spice pudding. It freezes really well and only needs ten minutes thawing time. Excellent!*

| | | |
|---|---|---|
| Large egg | 1 | 1 |
| Butter (or hard margarine), softened | 1/4 cup | 60 mL |
| Brown sugar, packed | 1/2 cup | 125 mL |
| Granulated sugar | 1/2 cup | 125 mL |
| Sour cream | 1/4 cup | 60 mL |
| Vanilla extract | 1 tsp. | 5 mL |
| Chopped walnuts | 1/2 cup | 125 mL |
| Coarsely chopped, fresh (or frozen) cranberries | 1/2 cup | 125 mL |
| Coarsely chopped, peeled cooking apple (such as McIntosh) | 1/2 cup | 125 mL |
| All-purpose flour | 1 cup | 250 mL |
| Baking powder | 1 tsp. | 5 mL |
| Ground cinnamon | 1/4 tsp. | 1 mL |
| Salt | 1/4 tsp. | 1 mL |
| CINNAMON SUGAR | | |
| Granulated sugar | 1 tbsp. | 15 mL |
| Ground cinnamon | 1/2 tsp. | 2 mL |

Beat first 4 ingredients in medium bowl until smooth. Add sour cream and vanilla. Beat well. Add next 3 ingredients. Stir.

Combine next 4 ingredients in small bowl. Add to cranberry mixture. Stir well. Spread evenly in greased 9 x 9 inch (22 x 22 cm) pan.

**Cinnamon Sugar:** Stir sugar into cinnamon in small bowl. Sprinkle over batter in pan. Bake in 350°F (175°C) oven for about 30 minutes until wooden pick inserted in centre comes out clean. Cuts into 36 squares.

*__1 square:__ 65 Calories; 2.8 g Total Fat (0.5 g Mono, 0.9 g Poly, 1.1 g Sat); 10 mg Cholesterol; 9 g Carbohydrate; trace Fibre; 1 g Protein; 44 mg Sodium*

Pictured on page 108.

# Chewy Nut Bars

*These have a caramel flavour combined with chocolate chips. Chewy.*

| | | |
|---|---|---|
| **Butter (or hard margarine)** | **1/2 cup** | **125 mL** |
| **Brown sugar, packed** | **1 cup** | **250 mL** |
| **Vanilla extract** | **1/2 tsp.** | **2 mL** |
| **Large egg** | **1** | **1** |
| **All-purpose flour** | **1 1/4 cups** | **300 mL** |
| **Baking powder** | **1 tsp.** | **5 mL** |
| **Salt** | **1/4 tsp.** | **1 mL** |
| **Semi-sweet chocolate chips** | **1/2 cup** | **125 mL** |
| **Finely chopped walnuts** | **1/4 cup** | **60 mL** |
| **ICING** | | |
| **Brown sugar, packed** | **1/3 cup** | **75 mL** |
| **Butter (or hard margarine)** | **3 tbsp.** | **50 mL** |
| **Milk** | **1 1/2 tbsp.** | **25 mL** |
| **Icing (confectioner's) sugar** | **1 cup** | **250 mL** |

Melt butter in small saucepan on medium. Remove from heat. Add brown sugar and vanilla. Stir. Add egg. Beat well.

Combine next 3 ingredients in medium bowl. Add butter mixture. Stir. Spread evenly in greased 8 x 8 inch (20 x 20 cm) pan.

Sprinkle chocolate chips and walnuts over top. Press down gently. Bake in 350°F (175°C) oven for about 35 minutes until wooden pick inserted in centre comes out clean. Let stand in pan on wire rack until cool.

**Icing:** Combine first 3 ingredients in small saucepan. Heat and stir on medium until melted. Bring to a boil. Reduce heat to medium-low. Simmer, uncovered, for 2 minutes, stirring occasionally. Transfer to medium bowl. Cool for about 30 minutes until lukewarm.

Add icing sugar. Beat until light and creamy, adding more milk or icing sugar as necessary until spreading consistency. Spread evenly over bottom layer. Cuts into 25 squares.

***1 square:*** *155 Calories; 7.0 g Total Fat (1.8 g Mono, 0.8 g Poly, 3.9 g Sat); 22 mg Cholesterol; 23 g Carbohydrate; trace Fibre; 1 g Protein; 89 mg Sodium*

Pictured on page 108.

# Three Layer Slice

*The top layer completes this square—nothing more is needed after baking.*

| | | |
|---|---|---|
| **FIRST LAYER** | | |
| All-purpose flour | 2 cups | 500 mL |
| Butter (or hard margarine), softened | 1/2 cup | 125 mL |
| Granulated sugar | 3 tbsp. | 50 mL |
| Salt | 1/2 tsp. | 2 mL |
| **SECOND LAYER** | | |
| Egg yolks (large) | 3 | 3 |
| Brown sugar, packed | 1 cup | 250 mL |
| Raisins (or currants) | 1 cup | 250 mL |
| All-purpose flour | 3/4 cup | 175 mL |
| Milk | 1/2 cup | 125 mL |
| Butter (or hard margarine), softened | 1/4 cup | 60 mL |
| Baking powder | 1 tbsp. | 15 mL |
| Vanilla extract | 1 tsp. | 5 mL |
| **THIRD LAYER** | | |
| Egg whites (large) | 3 | 3 |
| Brown sugar, packed | 1 cup | 250 mL |
| Medium unsweetened coconut | 1 cup | 250 mL |
| Vanilla extract | 1 tsp. | 5 mL |

**First Layer:** Mix all 4 ingredients in medium bowl until crumbly. Press firmly into ungreased 9 x 13 inch (22 x 33 cm) pan. Bake in 350°F (175°C) oven for 10 minutes.

**Second Layer:** Combine all 8 ingredients in separate medium bowl. Pour over first layer. Bake for 20 to 25 minutes until set.

**Third Layer:** Combine all 4 ingredients in small bowl. Spread evenly over second layer. Bake for about 15 minutes until golden. Let stand in pan on wire rack until cool. Cuts into 54 squares.

***1 square:*** *101 Calories; 3.7 g Total Fat (0.8 g Mono, 0.1 g Poly, 2.5 g Sat); 18 mg Cholesterol; 16 g Carbohydrate; trace Fibre; 1 g Protein; 79 mg Sodium*

Pictured on page 108.

# Nutted Gumdrops

*It's a sweet surprise to find out what you thought was fruit is actually candy.*

| | | |
|---|---|---|
| Large egg | 1 | 1 |
| Butter (or hard margarine), softened | 1/2 cup | 125 mL |
| Granulated sugar | 1/2 cup | 125 mL |
| Vanilla extract | 1 tsp. | 5 mL |
| Finely chopped gumdrops (no black) | 1 cup | 250 mL |
| Evaporated milk (or half-and-half cream) | 3/4 cup | 175 mL |
| All-purpose flour | 1 cup | 250 mL |
| Chopped walnuts | 1/2 cup | 125 mL |
| Baking powder | 1 tsp. | 5 mL |
| Salt | 1/2 tsp. | 2 mL |
| ICING | | |
| Icing (confectioner's) sugar | 1 1/2 cups | 375 mL |
| Butter (or hard margarine), softened | 2 tbsp. | 30 mL |
| Evaporated milk (or half-and-half cream) | 1 1/2 tbsp. | 25 mL |
| Vanilla extract | 1/2 tsp. | 2 mL |

Beat first 4 ingredients in large bowl until smooth. Add gumdrops and evaporated milk. Stir.

Combine next 4 ingredients in medium bowl. Add to gumdrop mixture. Stir well. Spread evenly in greased 9 x 9 inch (22 x 22 cm) pan. Bake in 350°F (175°C) oven for 25 to 30 minutes until golden. Cool slightly.

**Icing:** Beat all 4 ingredients in medium bowl until smooth, adding more milk or icing sugar as necessary until spreading consistency. Spread evenly over warm bottom layer. Cuts into 36 squares.

***1 square:*** *110 Calories; 4.8 g Total Fat (1.1 g Mono, 0.9 g Poly, 2.4 g Sat); 16 mg Cholesterol; 16 g Carbohydrate; trace Fibre; 1 g Protein; 80 mg Sodium*

Pictured on page 108.

### *Paré Pointer*

*Go ahead and eat all those goodies. No point in looking like a dream—you will just give someone insomnia!*

# Cranberry Squares

*A pretty square that tastes as good as it looks. Nice and chewy.*

| | | |
|---|---|---|
| **BOTTOM LAYER** | | |
| All-purpose flour | 1 1/2 cups | 375 mL |
| Brown sugar, packed | 1/2 cup | 125 mL |
| Butter (or hard margarine), softened | 1/2 cup | 125 mL |
| Salt | 1/8 tsp. | 0.5 mL |
| **FILLING** | | |
| Large eggs | 2 | 2 |
| Granulated sugar | 1 cup | 250 mL |
| Whole cranberry sauce, any excess liquid drained | 3/4 cup | 175 mL |
| Chopped raisins (or currants) | 1/2 cup | 125 mL |
| Medium unsweetened coconut | 1/2 cup | 125 mL |
| All-purpose flour | 1/3 cup | 75 mL |
| Baking powder | 1 tsp. | 5 mL |
| Salt | 1/4 tsp. | 1 mL |
| **ICING** | | |
| Icing (confectioner's) sugar | 1 1/2 cups | 375 mL |
| Butter (or hard margarine) | 3 tbsp. | 50 mL |
| Milk (or water) | 1 1/2 tbsp. | 25 mL |
| Vanilla extract | 1/2 tsp. | 2 mL |

**Bottom Layer:** Mix all 4 ingredients in large bowl until crumbly. Press firmly into ungreased 8 x 8 inch (20 x 20 cm) pan. Bake in 350°F (175°C) oven for 10 minutes.

**Filling:** Beat eggs in same large bowl until frothy. Add remaining 7 ingredients. Mix well. Spread evenly over bottom layer. Bake for about 30 minutes until wooden pick inserted in centre comes out clean. Let stand in pan on wire rack until cool.

**Icing:** Beat all 4 ingredients in small bowl until smooth, adding more milk or icing sugar as necessary until spreading consistency. Spread evenly over filling. Cuts into 25 squares.

***1 square:*** *188 Calories; 6.4 g Total Fat (1.5 g Mono, 0.3 g Poly, 4.1 g Sat); 30 mg Cholesterol; 32 g Carbohydrate; 1 g Fibre; 2 g Protein; 103 mg Sodium*

Pictured on page 125.

# Chewy Candy Bars

*For an extra rich treat, this chewy square fits the bill.*

| | | |
|---|---|---|
| **BOTTOM LAYER** | | |
| Large egg | 1 | 1 |
| Brown sugar, packed | 1 cup | 250 mL |
| Butter (or hard margarine), softened | 1/2 cup | 125 mL |
| Vanilla extract | 1/2 tsp. | 2 mL |
| Quick-cooking rolled oats | 1 cup | 250 mL |
| All-purpose flour | 3/4 cup | 175 mL |
| Baking soda | 1/2 tsp. | 2 mL |
| Salt | 1/2 tsp. | 2 mL |
| **SECOND LAYER** | | |
| Sweetened condensed milk | 2/3 cup | 150 mL |
| Cream cheese, softened | 4 oz. | 125 g |
| Vanilla extract | 1/2 tsp. | 2 mL |
| Finely chopped walnuts | 1/2 cup | 125 mL |
| **TOPPING** | | |
| Semi-sweet chocolate chips | 1/3 cup | 75 mL |
| Reserved cream cheese mixture | 3 tbsp. | 50 mL |
| Milk | 2 tsp. | 10 mL |

**Bottom Layer:** Beat first 4 ingredients in large bowl until smooth. Add next 4 ingredients. Mix well. Press firmly into greased 9 x 9 inch (22 x 22 cm) pan.

**Second Layer:** Beat first 3 ingredients in small bowl. Reserve 3 tbsp. (50 mL) in small saucepan. Spread remaining cream cheese mixture evenly over bottom layer.

Sprinkle walnuts over top. Bake in 350°F (175°C) oven for about 25 minutes until set.

**Topping:** Add chocolate chips to reserved cream cheese mixture in saucepan. Heat on lowest heat until chocolate chips are melted, adding milk 1 tsp. (5 mL) at a time, until barely pourable consistency. Immediately drizzle over second layer. Let stand in pan on wire rack until cool. Cuts into 36 squares.

***1 square:*** *114 Calories; 5.9 g Total Fat (1.0 g Mono, 0.9 g Poly, 3.1 g Sat); 17 mg Cholesterol; 14 g Carbohydrate; 1 g Fibre; 2 g Protein; 90 mg Sodium*

Pictured on page 125.

# Lemon Squares

*A simple recipe for lemon lovers.*

| | | |
|---|---|---|
| **BOTTOM LAYER** | | |
| **All-purpose flour** | **1 1/2 cups** | **375 mL** |
| **Butter (or hard margarine), softened** | **1/2 cup** | **125 mL** |
| **Granulated sugar** | **1/4 cup** | **60 mL** |
| **SECOND LAYER** | | |
| **Large eggs** | **2** | **2** |
| **Granulated sugar** | **1 cup** | **250 mL** |
| **Medium unsweetened coconut** | **1 cup** | **250 mL** |
| **Lemon juice** | **3 tbsp.** | **50 mL** |
| **All-purpose flour** | **2 tbsp.** | **30 mL** |
| **Baking powder** | **1/2 tsp.** | **2 mL** |
| **Salt** | **1/4 tsp.** | **1 mL** |
| **LEMON ICING** | | |
| **Icing (confectioner's) sugar** | **1 1/2 cups** | **375 mL** |
| **Butter (or hard margarine), softened** | **2 tbsp.** | **30 mL** |
| **Lemon juice** | **4 tsp.** | **20 mL** |

**Bottom Layer:** Mix all 3 ingredients in small bowl until crumbly. Press firmly into ungreased 9 x 9 inch (22 x 22 cm) pan. Bake in 350°F (175°C) oven for 15 minutes.

**Second Layer:** Beat eggs with a fork in large bowl. Add next 6 ingredients. Stir. Spread evenly over bottom layer. Bake for about 30 minutes until golden brown. Let stand in pan on wire rack until cool.

**Lemon Icing:** Beat all 3 ingredients in small bowl until smooth, adding more lemon juice or icing sugar as necessary until spreading consistency. Spread evenly over second layer. Cuts into 36 squares.

*__1 square:__ 111 Calories; 4.8 g Total Fat (1.0 g Mono, 0.2 g Poly, 3.3 g Sat); 20 mg Cholesterol; 17 g Carbohydrate; trace Fibre; 1 g Protein; 51 mg Sodium*

Pictured on page 125.

# Raspberry Smacks

*A rich, sticky square for special occasions.*

| | | |
|---|---|---|
| **BOTTOM LAYER** | | |
| **Egg yolks (large)** | **2** | **2** |
| **All-purpose flour** | **1 1/2 cups** | **375 mL** |
| **Brown sugar, packed** | **1/2 cup** | **125 mL** |
| **Butter (or hard margarine), softened** | **1/2 cup** | **125 mL** |
| **Baking powder** | **1 tsp.** | **5 mL** |
| **Vanilla extract** | **1 tsp.** | **5 mL** |
| **Salt** | **1/4 tsp.** | **1 mL** |
| **FILLING** | | |
| **Raspberry jam** | **1 cup** | **250 mL** |
| **TOP LAYER** | | |
| **Egg whites (large), room temperature** | **2** | **2** |
| **Brown sugar, packed** | **1 cup** | **250 mL** |
| **Chopped walnuts (optional)** | **1/2 cup** | **125 mL** |

**Bottom Layer:** Mix all 7 ingredients in large bowl until crumbly. Press firmly into ungreased 9 x 9 inch (22 x 22 cm) pan.

**Filling:** Drop teaspoonfuls of jam, in dabs here and there, over bottom layer. Spread evenly.

**Top Layer:** Beat egg whites in medium bowl until frothy. Add brown sugar, 1/3 cup (75 mL) at a time, beating well after each addition until stiff peaks form. Fold in walnuts. Spread evenly over filling. Bake in 350°F (175°C) oven for about 25 minutes until golden. Let stand in pan on wire rack until cool. Cuts into 36 squares.

*__1 square:__ 100 Calories; 2.8 g Total Fat (0.8 g Mono, 0.1 g Poly, 1.7 g Sat); 18 mg Cholesterol; 19 g Carbohydrate; trace Fibre; 1 g Protein; 56 mg Sodium*

Pictured on page 125.

### *Paré Pointer*

*Anything consumed while suffering a cold doesn't count—if you can't taste it you can't absorb it.*

# Orange Date Bars

*The dates keep these moist as well as lending their unique flavour.*

| | | |
|---|---|---|
| Large egg | 1 | 1 |
| Butter (or hard margarine), melted | 1/2 cup | 125 mL |
| Granulated sugar | 1/2 cup | 125 mL |
| Orange juice | 3 tbsp. | 50 mL |
| Grated orange zest | 1 tsp. | 5 mL |
| All-purpose flour | 1 cup | 250 mL |
| Baking soda | 1/2 tsp. | 2 mL |
| Chopped pitted dates | 1/2 cup | 125 mL |
| Chopped walnuts | 1/2 cup | 125 mL |
| ICING | | |
| Icing (confectioner's) sugar | 1 1/2 cups | 375 mL |
| Butter (or hard margarine), softened | 2 tbsp. | 30 mL |
| Grated orange zest | 1 tsp. | 5 mL |
| Orange juice | 1 1/2 tbsp. | 25 mL |

Beat first 5 ingredients in large bowl until combined.

Mix flour and baking soda in small bowl. Add to orange juice mixture. Stir.

Add dates and walnuts. Stir well. Spread evenly in greased 9 x 9 inch (22 x 22 cm) pan. Bake in 350°F (175°C) oven for about 20 minutes until wooden pick inserted in centre comes out clean. Let stand in pan on wire rack until cool.

**Icing:** Beat all 4 ingredients in medium bowl until smooth, adding more orange juice or icing sugar as necessary until spreading consistency. Spread evenly over bottom layer. Cuts into 36 squares.

***1 square:*** *90 Calories; 4.4 g Total Fat (1.0 g Mono, 0.9 g Poly, 2.1 g Sat); 14 mg Cholesterol; 12 g Carbohydrate; trace Fibre; 1 g Protein; 42 mg Sodium*

Pictured on page 125.

## Paré Pointer

*Eat more and live longer. Look at the whale and the elephant. Eat like a fly and you're dead in two weeks!*

# Grant's Special

*My son's favourite square, also known as Seafoam Chews. Cover to soften meringue for easier cutting.*

| | | |
|---|---|---|
| Egg yolks (large) | 2 | 2 |
| All-purpose flour | 2 cups | 500 mL |
| Brown sugar, packed | 1/2 cup | 125 mL |
| Butter (or hard margarine), softened | 1/2 cup | 125 mL |
| Granulated sugar | 1/2 cup | 125 mL |
| Milk | 3 tbsp. | 50 mL |
| Baking powder | 2 tsp. | 10 mL |
| Baking soda | 1 tsp. | 5 mL |
| Vanilla extract | 1 tsp. | 5 mL |
| Salt | 1/2 tsp. | 2 mL |
| Semi-sweet chocolate chips | 1 cup | 250 mL |
| Egg whites (large), room temperature | 2 | 2 |
| Brown sugar, packed | 1 cup | 250 mL |
| Chopped salted peanuts | 3/4 cup | 175 mL |

Mix first 10 ingredients in large bowl until crumbly. Press firmly into ungreased 9 x 9 inch (22 x 22 cm) pan.

Sprinkle chocolate chips evenly over top.

Beat egg whites in medium bowl until frothy. Add brown sugar, 1/3 cup (75 mL) at a time, beating well after each addition until stiff peaks form. Drop by teaspoonfuls, in dabs here and there, over chocolate chips. Spread evenly.

Sprinkle peanuts over top. Press down gently. Bake in 350°F (175°C) oven for about 35 minutes until golden. Let stand in pan on wire rack until cool. Cuts into 36 squares.

***1 square:*** *140 Calories; 6.0 g Total Fat (1.2 g Mono, 0.2 g Poly, 3.0 g Sat); 18 mg Cholesterol; 20 g Carbohydrate; 1 g Fibre; 2 g Protein; 144 mg Sodium*

Pictured on page 125.

# Lemon Crumb Squares

*The cracker crumbs in the bottom layer give this a different twist.*

| | | |
|---|---|---|
| **BOTTOM LAYER** | | |
| **Butter (or hard margarine)** | **3/4 cup** | **175 mL** |
| **Graham cracker crumbs** | **1 3/4 cups** | **425 mL** |
| **All-purpose flour** | **3/4 cup** | **175 mL** |
| **Granulated sugar** | **1/2 cup** | **125 mL** |
| **Medium unsweetened coconut** | **1/2 cup** | **125 mL** |
| **TOP LAYER** | | |
| **Large egg** | **1** | **1** |
| **Fine coconut** | **1/2 cup** | **125 mL** |
| **Granulated sugar** | **1/2 cup** | **125 mL** |
| **Lemon juice** | **1/4 cup** | **60 mL** |
| **Grated lemon zest (see Tip, page 60)** | **2 tsp.** | **10 mL** |

**Bottom Layer:** Melt butter in medium saucepan on medium. Remove from heat. Stir in next 4 ingredients. Press 2/3 of crumb mixture firmly into ungreased 9 x 9 inch (22 x 22 cm) pan. Reserve remaining crumb mixture.

**Top Layer:** Combine all 5 ingredients in small, heavy saucepan. Heat on medium for about 5 minutes, stirring constantly, until thickened. Spread evenly over bottom layer. Sprinkle with reserved crumb mixture. Press down gently. Bake in 350°F (175°C) oven for 25 to 30 minutes until golden brown. Let stand in pan on wire rack until cool. Cuts into 36 squares.

***1 square:** 99 Calories; 5.8 g Total Fat (1.2 g Mono, 0.3 g Poly, 3.8 g Sat); 16 mg Cholesterol; 11 g Carbohydrate; trace Fibre; 1 g Protein; 54 mg Sodium*

Pictured on page 125.

### *Paré Pointer*

*Healthy size snacks taken at bedtime are really medication. Would you rather live on sleeping pills? Calorie count of zero.*

# Orange Coconut Chews

*A moist and chewy square with just a hint of orange.*

| | | |
|---|---|---|
| Butter (or hard margarine) | 1/2 cup | 125 mL |
| Large egg, fork-beaten | 1 | 1 |
| Brown sugar, packed | 1 cup | 250 mL |
| Chopped pitted dates | 1 cup | 250 mL |
| Medium unsweetened coconut | 1 cup | 250 mL |
| Grated orange zest | 2 tsp. | 10 mL |
| Vanilla extract | 1 tsp. | 5 mL |
| All-purpose flour | 1/2 cup | 125 mL |
| Baking powder | 1 tsp. | 5 mL |
| Salt | 1/2 tsp. | 2 mL |
| ICING | | |
| Icing (confectioner's) sugar | 1 1/2 cups | 375 mL |
| Butter (or hard margarine), softened | 2 tbsp. | 30 mL |
| Frozen concentrated orange juice, thawed | 1 1/2 tbsp. | 25 mL |

Melt butter in large saucepan on medium. Remove from heat. Add next 6 ingredients. Mix well.

Combine remaining 3 ingredients in small bowl. Add to coconut mixture. Stir well. Press firmly into greased 8 x 8 inch (20 x 20 cm) pan. Bake in 350°F (175°C) oven for about 30 minutes until wooden pick inserted in centre comes out clean. Let stand in pan on wire rack until cool.

**Icing:** Beat all 3 ingredients in small bowl until smooth, adding more orange juice or icing sugar as necessary until spreading consistency. Spread evenly over bottom layer. Cuts into 25 squares.

***1 square:*** *148 Calories; 5.7 g Total Fat (1.3 g Mono, 0.2 g Poly, 3.8 g Sat); 21 mg Cholesterol; 25 g Carbohydrate; 1 g Fibre; 1 g Protein; 115 mg Sodium*

Pictured on page 125.

## *Paré Pointer*

*Having a big snack at bedtime won't count against your diet if you plan to sleep through breakfast.*

# Ginger Bars

*Hints of ginger flavour fill this bar, yet there's not a speck of ginger in the recipe!*

| | | |
|---|---|---|
| Large egg | 1 | 1 |
| Brown sugar, packed | 1/2 cup | 125 mL |
| Butter (or hard margarine), softened | 1/2 cup | 125 mL |
| Fancy (mild) molasses | 1/2 cup | 125 mL |
| All-purpose flour | 2 cups | 500 mL |
| Chopped walnuts | 1/2 cup | 125 mL |
| Coarsely chopped raisins (or currants) | 1/2 cup | 125 mL |
| Milk | 1/2 cup | 125 mL |
| Baking powder | 1 1/2 tsp. | 7 mL |
| Vanilla extract | 1/2 tsp. | 2 mL |
| Salt | 1/4 tsp. | 1 mL |
| VANILLA ICING | | |
| Icing (confectioner's) sugar | 1 1/2 cups | 375 mL |
| Butter (or hard margarine), softened | 3 tbsp. | 50 mL |
| Milk | 1 1/2 tbsp. | 25 mL |
| Vanilla extract | 1/2 tsp. | 2 mL |

Beat first 3 ingredients in large bowl until smooth. Add molasses. Beat well.

Add next 7 ingredients. Stir well. Spread evenly in greased 9 x 9 inch (22 x 22 cm) pan. Bake in 350°F (175°C) oven for about 30 minutes, until wooden pick inserted in centre comes out clean. Cool slightly.

**Vanilla Icing:** Beat all 4 ingredients in small bowl until smooth, adding more milk or icing sugar as necessary until spreading consistency. Spread evenly over warm bottom layer. Let stand in pan until icing is set. Cuts into 36 squares.

*__1 square:__ 120 Calories; 4.8 g Total Fat (1.1 g Mono, 0.9 g Poly, 2.4 g Sat); 15 mg Cholesterol; 19 g Carbohydrate; trace Fibre; 1 g Protein; 71 mg Sodium*

Pictured on page 125.

# Chocolate Chip Squares

*This is a moist, caramel-tasting square, with chocolate giving it an extra special touch.*

| | | |
|---|---|---|
| **Butter (or hard margarine), softened** | **1/2 cup** | **125 mL** |
| **Brown sugar, packed** | **1/2 cup** | **125 mL** |
| **Granulated sugar** | **1/4 cup** | **60 mL** |
| **Large egg** | **1** | **1** |
| **Vanilla extract** | **1 tsp.** | **5 mL** |
| **All-purpose flour** | **1 cup** | **250 mL** |
| **Baking soda** | **1/2 tsp.** | **2 mL** |
| **Salt** | **1/2 tsp.** | **2 mL** |
| **Semi-sweet chocolate chips** | **1 cup** | **250 mL** |
| **Chopped walnuts** | **1/2 cup** | **125 mL** |

Beat butter and both sugars in medium bowl. Add egg and vanilla. Beat well.

Combine next 3 ingredients in small bowl. Add to butter mixture. Stir.

Add chocolate chips and walnuts. Stir well. Spread evenly in greased 9 x 9 inch (22 x 22 cm) pan. Bake in 350°F (175°C) oven for 25 to 30 minutes until set and browned. Let stand in pan on wire rack until cool. Cuts into 36 squares.

***1 square:** 86 Calories; 5.2 g Total Fat (1.3 g Mono, 0.9 g Poly, 2.6 g Sat); 13 mg Cholesterol; 10 g Carbohydrate; trace Fibre; 1 g Protein; 71 mg Sodium*

Pictured on page 125.

## *Paré Pointer*

*Did you know that sampling a square or two before company comes (to see if it is all right to serve), doesn't count on your diet?*

# Magic Bars

V.V. good

*A simple trick that's quite amazing.*

| | | |
|---|---|---|
| **Butter (or hard margarine), melted** | **1/2 cup** | **125 mL** |
| **Graham cracker crumbs** | **1 1/2 cups** | **375 mL** |
| **Can of sweetened condensed milk** | **11 oz.** | **300 mL** |
| **Flaked coconut** | **1 1/3 cups** | **325 mL** |
| **Chopped walnuts** | **1 cup** | **250 mL** |
| **Semi-sweet chocolate chips** | **1 cup** | **250 mL** |

Spread melted butter evenly in 9 x 13 inch (22 x 22 cm) pan. Sprinkle with graham crumbs.

Drop teaspoonfuls of condensed milk, in dabs here and there, over crumb mixture. Spread evenly.

Sprinkle remaining 3 ingredients, in order given, over condensed milk. Press down gently. Bake in 350°F (175°C) oven for 25 to 30 minutes until golden brown. Let stand in pan on wire rack until cool. Cuts into 54 squares.

***1 square:*** *83 Calories; 5.3 g Total Fat (1.1 g Mono, 1.2 g Poly, 2.6 g Sat); 6 mg Cholesterol; 8 g Carbohydrate; trace Fibre; 1 g Protein; 38 mg Sodium*

Pictured on page 126.

**Variation:** Reduce chocolate chips to 1/2 cup (125 mL). Sprinkle with 1/2 cup (125 mL) butterscotch chips after chocolate chips.

1. Ginger Bars, page 122
2. Lemon Crumb Squares, page 120
3. Orange Coconut Chews, page 121
4. Cranberry Squares, page 114
5. Grant's Special, page 119
6. Raspberry Smacks, page 117
7. Orange Date Bars, page 118
8. Lemon Squares, page 116
9. Chocolate Chip Squares, page 123
10. Chewy Candy Bars, page 115
11. Chinese Chews, page 109

Props courtesy of: Cherison Enterprises Inc.

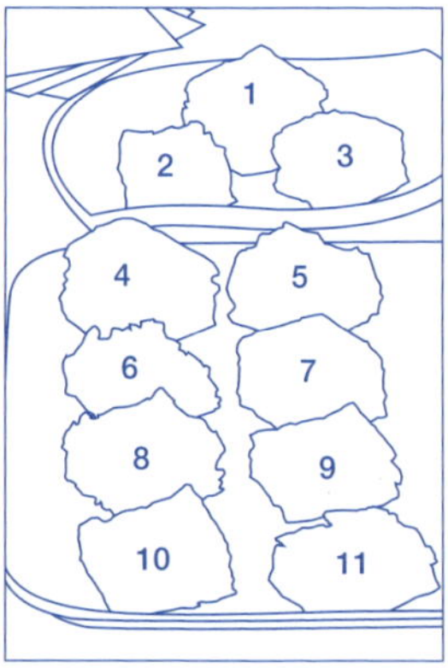

# Swirl Squares

*No need to make an icing for this square. The attractive swirl is made with the help of chocolate chips.*

| | | |
|---|---|---|
| Large egg | 1 | 1 |
| Brown sugar, packed | 1/2 cup | 125 mL |
| Butter (or hard margarine), softened | 1/2 cup | 125 mL |
| Granulated sugar | 1/4 cup | 60 mL |
| Vanilla extract | 1/2 tsp. | 2 mL |
| All-purpose flour | 1 1/8 cups | 280 mL |
| Chopped walnuts | 1/2 cup | 125 mL |
| Baking soda | 1/2 tsp. | 2 mL |
| Salt | 1/2 tsp. | 2 mL |
| Semi-sweet chocolate chips | 1 cup | 250 mL |

Beat first 5 ingredients in large bowl until smooth and creamy.

Combine next 4 ingredients in small bowl. Add to butter mixture. Stir. Spread evenly in greased 9 x 9 inch (22 x 22 cm) pan.

Sprinkle chocolate chips evenly over top. Bake in 375°F (190°C) oven for about 2 minutes, until chips are soft. Swirl knife through batter to create marble effect. Bake for about 20 minutes until wooden pick inserted in centre comes out clean. Let stand in pan on wire rack until cool. Cuts into 36 squares.

***1 square:** 87 Calories; 5.2 g Total Fat (1.3 g Mono, 0.9 g Poly, 2.6 g Sat); 13 mg Cholesterol; 10 g Carbohydrate; trace Fibre; 1 g Protein; 71 mg Sodium*

Pictured at left and on back cover.

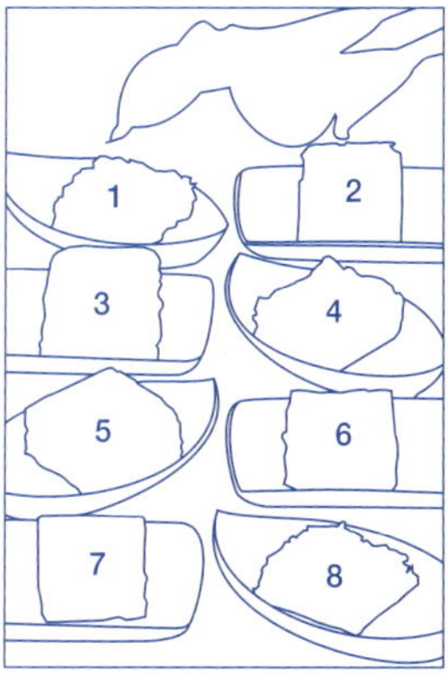


1. Magic Bars, page 124
2. Nut Smacks, page 129
3. Cinnamon Bars, page 132
4. Swirl Squares, above
5. Chocolate Peppermint Slice, page 128
6. Lemon Graham Slice, page 130
7. Caramel Shortbread, page 131
8. Chocolate Coconut Melts, page 130

# Chocolate Peppermint Slice

*A thin layer of peppermint provides a surprisingly refreshing taste that goes great with the chocolate icing.*

| | | |
|---|---|---|
| **BOTTOM LAYER** | | |
| **All-purpose flour** | **1 1/2 cups** | **350 mL** |
| **Medium unsweetened coconut** | **1 1/2 cups** | **350 mL** |
| **Butter (or hard margarine), softened** | **3/4 cup** | **175 mL** |
| **Brown sugar, packed** | **1/2 cup** | **125 mL** |
| **FILLING** | | |
| **Icing (confectioner's) sugar** | **1 1/2 cups** | **350 mL** |
| **Butter (or hard margarine), softened** | **2 tbsp.** | **30 mL** |
| **Milk** | **2 tbsp.** | **30 mL** |
| **Peppermint extract** | **1/2 tsp.** | **2 mL** |
| **TOP LAYER** | | |
| **Butter (or hard margarine)** | **6 tbsp.** | **100 mL** |
| **Chocolate milk powder** | **1/2 cup** | **125 mL** |

**Bottom Layer:** Mix all 4 ingredients in medium bowl until crumbly. Press firmly into ungreased 9 x 9 inch (22 x 22 cm) pan. Bake in 350°F (175°C) oven for 15 minutes. Let stand in pan until cooled completely.

**Filling:** Beat all 4 ingredients in separate medium bowl until smooth. Spread evenly over bottom layer.

**Top Layer:** Melt butter in small saucepan on medium. Remove from heat. Add chocolate milk powder. Stir. Transfer to small bowl. Cool to room temperature. Drop by teaspoonfuls, in dabs here and there, over filling. Spread evenly. Let stand in pan until set. Cuts into 36 squares.

***1 square:** 133 Calories; 8.8 g Total Fat (1.9 g Mono, 0.3 g Poly, 6.1 g Sat); 19 mg Cholesterol; 13 g Carbohydrate; 1 g Fibre; 1 g Protein; 54 mg Sodium*

Pictured on page 126.

## *Paré Pointer*

*In case of a natural disaster it is the duty of every citizen to have an extra supply of calories stored up.*

# Nut Smacks

*Butterscotch flavour, rich with nuts and brown sugar. An old family favourite. Covering pan allows meringue to soften for easier cutting.*

| | | |
|---|---|---|
| **BOTTOM LAYER** | | |
| Egg yolks (large) | 2 | 2 |
| All-purpose flour | 1 1/2 cups | 375 mL |
| Brown sugar, packed | 1/2 cup | 125 mL |
| Butter (or hard margarine), softened | 1/2 cup | 125 mL |
| Baking powder | 1 tsp. | 5 mL |
| Vanilla extract | 1 tsp. | 5 mL |
| Salt | 1/4 tsp. | 1 mL |
| **TOP LAYER** | | |
| Egg whites (large), room temperature | 2 | 2 |
| Brown sugar, packed | 1 cup | 250 mL |
| Chopped walnuts | 1 cup | 250 mL |

**Bottom Layer:** Mix all 7 ingredients in large bowl until crumbly. Press firmly into ungreased 9 x 9 inch (22 x 22 cm) pan.

**Top Layer:** Beat egg whites in medium bowl until frothy. Add brown sugar, 1/3 cup (75 mL) at a time, beating well after each addition until stiff peaks form. Fold in walnuts. Spread evenly over bottom layer. Bake in 350°F (175°C) oven for about 25 minutes until golden. Let stand in pan on wire rack until cool. Cuts into 36 squares.

***1 square:*** *100 Calories; 5.0 g Total Fat (1.1 g Mono, 1.7 g Poly, 1.9 g Sat); 18 mg Cholesterol; 13 g Carbohydrate; trace Fibre; 1 g Protein; 57 mg Sodium*

Pictured on page 126.

### Paré Pointer

*If you take your coffee without cream and sugar, any doughnuts you consume with it won't have a calorie in them.*

# Lemon Graham Slice

*With its exceptionally lemony flavour, this one is for lemon lovers.*

| | | |
|---|---|---|
| **BOTTOM LAYER** | | |
| **Butter (or hard margarine)** | **1/2 cup** | **125 mL** |
| **Graham cracker crumbs** | **1 1/2 cups** | **375 mL** |
| **Brown sugar, packed** | **1/3 cup** | **75 mL** |
| **Baking powder** | **1/2 tsp.** | **2 mL** |
| **Salt** | **1/8 tsp.** | **0.5 mL** |
| **TOP LAYER** | | |
| **Can of sweetened condensed milk** | **11 oz.** | **300 mL** |
| **Lemon juice** | **1/2 cup** | **125 mL** |
| **Vanilla extract** | **1 tsp.** | **5 mL** |

**Bottom Layer:** Melt butter in medium saucepan on medium. Remove from heat. Add remaining 4 ingredients. Stir. Mix well. Press firmly into ungreased 9 x 9 inch (22 x 22 cm) pan.

**Top Layer:** Combine all 3 ingredients in small bowl. Spread evenly over bottom layer. Bake in 350°F (175°C) oven for 20 to 25 minutes until set. Let stand in pan on wire rack until cool. Cuts into 36 squares.

***1 square:** 76 Calories; 3.6 g Total Fat (0.8 g Mono, 0.2 g Poly, 2.1 g Sat); 9 mg Cholesterol; 10 g Carbohydrate; trace Fibre; 1 g Protein; 66 mg Sodium*

Pictured on page 126.

# Chocolate Coconut Melts

*And yes, it does melt in your mouth.*

| | | |
|---|---|---|
| **Can of sweetened condensed milk** | **11 oz.** | **300 mL** |
| **Unsweetened chocolate baking squares (1 oz., 28 g, each), chopped** | **2** | **2** |
| **Salt** | **1/4 tsp.** | **1 mL** |
| **Flaked coconut** | **2 2/3 cups** | **650 mL** |
| **Vanilla extract** | **1 tsp.** | **5 mL** |

*(continued on next page)*

Combine first 3 ingredients in small, heavy saucepan. Heat and stir on medium-low until melted and thickened.

Add coconut and vanilla. Stir well. Spread evenly in greased 8 x 8 inch (20 x 20 cm) pan. Bake in 350°F (175°C) oven for about 20 minutes until set. Let stand in pan on wire rack until cool. Cuts into 25 squares.

***1 square:** 92 Calories; 4.7 g Total Fat (0.5 g Mono, trace Poly, 4 g Sat); 3 mg Cholesterol; 12 g Carbohydrate; 1 g Fibre; 2 g Protein; 59 mg Sodium*

Pictured on page 126.

# Caramel Shortbread

*A rich, toffee-like icing coats this delicate bottom layer.*

| | | |
|---|---|---|
| **BOTTOM LAYER** | | |
| **All-purpose flour** | **1 cup** | **250 mL** |
| **Butter (or hard margarine), softened** | **1/2 cup** | **125 mL** |
| **Icing (confectioner's) sugar** | **1/2 cup** | **125 mL** |
| **TOP LAYER** | | |
| **Sweetened condensed milk** | **2/3 cup** | **150 mL** |
| **Brown sugar, packed** | **1/2 cup** | **125 mL** |
| **Butter (or hard margarine)** | **1/2 cup** | **125 mL** |
| **Dark corn syrup** | **1/4 cup** | **60 mL** |

**Bottom Layer:** Mix all 3 ingredients in medium bowl until crumbly. Press firmly into ungreased 8 x 8 inch (20 x 20 cm) pan. Bake in 350°F (175°C) oven for about 15 minutes until edges start to turn golden.

**Top Layer:** Combine all 4 ingredients in large heavy saucepan. Bring to a boil on medium. Boil for 3 minutes, stirring constantly. Remove from heat. Stir vigorously for 1 minute. Pour over bottom layer. Spread evenly. Let stand in pan on wire rack for about 4 hours until cooled completely. Cuts into 25 squares.

***1 square:** 143 Calories; 7.9 g Total Fat (1.9 g Mono, 0.3 g Poly, 5.0 g Sat); 21 mg Cholesterol; 17 g Carbohydrate; trace Fibre; 1 g Protein; 68 mg Sodium*

Pictured on page 126.

**Note:** For easier cutting, invert onto plastic wrap and cut. Turn right side up.

# Cinnamon Bars

*This spicy bar offers a welcomed warmth.*

| | | |
|---|---|---|
| **BOTTOM LAYER** | | |
| **Egg yolk (large)** | **1** | **1** |
| **All-purpose flour** | **1 1/2 cups** | **375 mL** |
| **Butter (or hard margarine), softened** | **1/2 cup** | **125 mL** |
| **Granulated sugar** | **1/3 cup** | **75 mL** |
| **Baking powder** | **1/2 tsp.** | **2 mL** |
| **Ground cinnamon** | **1 1/2 tsp.** | **7 mL** |
| **Salt** | **1/8 tsp.** | **0.5 mL** |
| **SECOND LAYER** | | |
| **Egg white (large), room temperature** | **1** | **1** |
| **Granulated sugar** | **1/2 cup** | **125 mL** |
| **Chopped walnuts** | **1/2 cup** | **125 mL** |
| **ICING** | | |
| **Brown sugar, packed** | **1/2 cup** | **125 mL** |
| **Butter (or hard margarine)** | **1/4 cup** | **60 mL** |
| **Milk** | **2 tbsp.** | **30 mL** |
| **Icing (confectioner's) sugar** | **1 cup** | **250 mL** |

**Bottom Layer:** Mix all 7 ingredients in large bowl until crumbly. Press firmly into ungreased 8 x 8 inch (20 x 20 cm) pan.

**Second Layer:** Beat egg white in medium bowl until frothy. Slowly add sugar, 1/4 cup (60 mL) at a time, beating well after each addition until stiff peaks form. Fold in walnuts. Spread evenly over bottom layer. Bake in 350°F (175°C) oven for about 25 minutes until golden. Let stand in pan on wire rack until cool.

**Icing:** Combine first 3 ingredients in small saucepan. Heat and stir on medium until melted. Bring to a boil. Reduce heat to medium-low. Simmer, uncovered, for 2 minutes, stirring occasionally. Transfer to medium bowl. Cool for about 30 minutes until lukewarm.

Add icing sugar. Beat until light and creamy, adding more milk or icing sugar as necessary until spreading consistency. Spread evenly over second layer. Cuts into 25 squares.

***1 square:** 153 Calories; 7.2 g Total Fat (1.7 g Mono, 1.4 g Poly, 3.7 g Sat); 23 mg Cholesterol; 22 g Carbohydrate; trace Fibre; 1 g Protein; 66 mg Sodium*

Pictured on page 126.

# Bikini Bars

*Itsy-bitsy, teeny-weeny bits of dates, walnuts and cherries fill this attractive square.*

| | | |
|---|---|---|
| **BOTTOM LAYER** | | |
| Medium unsweetened coconut | 2 1/2 cups | 625 mL |
| Chopped pitted dates | 2 cups | 500 mL |
| Sweetened condensed milk | 2/3 cup | 150 mL |
| Chopped walnuts | 1/2 cup | 125 mL |
| Chopped maraschino cherries, well drained | 1/4 cup | 60 mL |
| Vanilla extract | 1 tsp. | 5 mL |
| Salt | 1/8 tsp. | 0.5 mL |
| **ICING** | | |
| Icing (confectioner's) sugar | 1 1/2 cups | 375 mL |
| Butter (or hard margarine), softened | 3 tbsp. | 50 mL |
| Milk | 1 1/2 tbsp. | 25 mL |
| Vanilla extract | 1/2 tsp. | 2 mL |
| **TOPPING** | | |
| Unsweetened chocolate baking square (1 oz., 28 g), chopped | 1 | 1 |

**Bottom Layer:** Combine first 7 ingredients in large bowl. Press firmly into greased 9 x 9 inch (22 x 22 cm) pan. Bake in 350°F (175°C) oven for about 30 minutes until set. Let stand in pan on wire rack until cool.

**Icing:** Beat all 4 ingredients in small bowl until smooth, adding more milk or icing sugar as necessary until spreading consistency. Spread evenly over bottom layer.

**Topping:** Heat chocolate in small, heavy saucepan on lowest heat until almost melted. Remove from heat. Stir until smooth. Drizzle over icing. Let stand in pan until set. Cuts into 36 squares.

***1 square:** 127 Calories; 6.2 g Total Fat (0.7 g Mono, 0.9 g Poly, 4.2 g Sat); 4 mg Cholesterol; 18 g Carbohydrate; 2 g Fibre; 1 g Protein; 25 mg Sodium*

Pictured on divider page.

# Butterscotch Toffee Bars

*A popular candy is the secret to the toffee layer.*

| | | |
|---|---|---|
| **BOTTOM LAYER** | | |
| All-purpose flour | 1 cup | 250 mL |
| Butter (or hard margarine), softened | 1/2 cup | 125 mL |
| Brown sugar, packed | 6 tbsp. | 100 mL |
| Salt | 1/8 tsp. | 0.5 mL |
| **TOP LAYER** | | |
| Butterscotch toffee pieces, (6 oz., 170 g, bag) | 1 | 1 |
| Butter (or hard margarine) | 2 tbsp. | 30 mL |
| Corn syrup | 1 tbsp. | 15 mL |
| Water | 1 tbsp. | 15 mL |
| Salt | 1/8 tsp. | 0.5 mL |
| Chopped walnuts | 2/3 cup | 150 mL |

**Bottom Layer:** Mix all 4 ingredients in medium bowl until crumbly. Press firmly into ungreased 9 x 9 inch (22 x 22 cm) pan. Bake in 375°F (190°C) oven for 10 minutes.

**Top Layer:** Heat first 5 ingredients in small, heavy saucepan on low, stirring often, until toffee pieces are melted.

Add walnuts. Stir. Spread evenly over bottom layer. Bake for 10 minutes. Let stand in pan on wire rack until cool. Cuts into 25 squares.

***1 square:*** *122 Calories; 7.4 g Total Fat (1.5 g Mono, 1.7 g Poly, 3.5 g Sat); 16 mg Cholesterol; 13 g Carbohydrate; trace Fibre; 1 g Protein; 94 mg Sodium*

Pictured on page 143.

## Paré Pointer

*At your next coffee party, anything consumed while your mind is busy with other things such as guests, coats, etc., cannot be absorbed.*

# Caramel Toffee Squares

*Now these are a real treat. Make this one of the first recipes to try.*

| | | |
|---|---|---|
| **BOTTOM LAYER** | | |
| **All-purpose flour** | **1 1/4 cups** | **300 mL** |
| **Butter, softened** | **2/3 cup** | **150 mL** |
| **Granulated sugar** | **1/4 cup** | **60 mL** |
| **SECOND LAYER** | | |
| **Butter (or hard margarine)** | **1/2 cup** | **125 mL** |
| **Brown sugar, packed** | **1/2 cup** | **125 ml** |
| **Corn syrup** | **2 tbsp.** | **30 mL** |
| **Sweetened condensed milk** | **1/2 cup** | **125 mL** |
| **TOP LAYER** | | |
| **Semi-sweet chocolate chips** | **1 1/2 cups** | **375 mL** |
| **Butter** | **1/4 cup** | **60 mL** |

**Bottom Layer:** Mix all 3 ingredients in medium bowl until crumbly. Press firmly into ungreased 9 x 9 inch (22 x 22 cm) pan. Bake in 350°F (175°C) oven for 15 minutes.

**Second Layer:** Combine all 4 ingredients in medium, heavy saucepan. Bring to a boil on medium. Boil for 3 minutes, stirring constantly. Remove from heat. Stir vigorously for 1 minute. Pour over bottom layer. Spread evenly. Let stand in pan on wire rack for 30 minutes.

**Top Layer:** Heat chocolate chips and butter in small, heavy saucepan on lowest heat until almost melted. Remove from heat. Stir until smooth. Spread evenly over second layer. Let stand in pan on wire rack for about 3 hours until set. Cuts into 36 squares.

***1 square:*** *145 Calories; 9.6 g Total Fat (2.6 g Mono, 0.3 g Poly, 6.0 g Sat); 20 mg Cholesterol; 15 g Carbohydrate; trace Fibre; 1 g Protein; 60 mg Sodium*

Pictured on page 143.

## *Paré Pointer*

*Help yourself to someone else's candy. No calories here since they are the ones that shouldn't have bought them.*

# Brownies

*Not only is this the easiest and fastest baked brownie to make, it's also one of the best tasting.*

| | | |
|---|---|---|
| Butter (or hard margarine) | 1/2 cup | 125 mL |
| Cocoa, sifted if lumpy | 1/4 cup | 60 mL |
| Large eggs | 2 | 2 |
| Granulated sugar | 1 cup | 250 mL |
| All-purpose flour | 3/4 cup | 175 mL |
| Chopped walnuts | 1/2 cup | 125 mL |
| Salt | 1/8 tsp. | 0.5 mL |
| ICING | | |
| Icing (confectioner's) sugar | 1 1/3 cups | 325 mL |
| Cocoa, sifted if lumpy | 1/3 cup | 75 mL |
| Butter (or hard margarine), softened | 3 tbsp. | 50 mL |
| Hot strong prepared coffee | 1 1/2 tbsp. | 25 mL |

Heat butter and cocoa in small, heavy saucepan on low, stirring occasionally, until smooth.

Beat eggs in medium bowl until frothy. Add next 4 ingredients and cocoa mixture. Stir well. Spread evenly in greased 8 x 8 inch (20 x 20 cm) pan. Bake in 350°F (175°C) oven for 25 to 30 minutes, until edges show signs of pulling away from sides of pan and wooden pick inserted in centre comes out moist but not wet with batter. Do not overbake. Cool slightly.

**Icing:** Beat all 4 ingredients in medium bowl until smooth, adding more coffee or icing sugar as necessary until spreading consistency. Spread evenly over warm brownie layer. Cuts into 25 squares.

*__1 square:__ 141 Calories; 7.1 g Total Fat (1.5 g Mono, 1.32 g Poly, 3.4 g Sat); 30 mg Cholesterol; 19 g Carbohydrate; 1 g Fibre; 2 g Protein; 52 mg Sodium*

Pictured on page 143.

### *Paré Pointer*

*Any food eaten during an intimate candlelight meal doesn't contain calories. It can't be starch, it's seduction.*

# Sesame Squares

*These squares have a chewy texture and a nutty taste.*

| | | |
|---|---|---|
| **BOTTOM LAYER** | | |
| **Large egg** | **1** | **1** |
| **All-purpose flour** | **1 1/2 cups** | **375 mL** |
| **Brown sugar, packed** | **1/2 cup** | **125 mL** |
| **Butter (or hard margarine), softened** | **1/2 cup** | **125 mL** |
| **FILLING** | | |
| **Raspberry (or apricot) jam** | **1 cup** | **250 mL** |
| **TOP LAYER** | | |
| **Large eggs** | **2** | **2** |
| **Brown sugar, packed** | **1 cup** | **250 mL** |
| **Sesame seeds, toasted (see Tip)** | **1/2 cup** | **125 mL** |
| **All-purpose flour** | **1 tbsp.** | **15 mL** |

**Bottom Layer:** Mix all 4 ingredients in large bowl until crumbly. Press firmly into ungreased 9 x 9 inch (22 x 22 cm) pan. Bake in 350°F (175°C) oven for 10 minutes. Let stand for 10 minutes.

**Filling:** Drop teaspoonfuls of jam, in dabs here and there, over warm bottom layer. Spread evenly.

**Top Layer:** Beat eggs and brown sugar in medium bowl. Add sesame seeds and flour. Stir well. Spread evenly over filling. Bake for about 25 minutes until set and golden. Let stand in pan on wire rack until cool. Cuts into 36 squares.

*__1 square:__ 116 Calories; 3.8 g Total Fat (0.7 g Mono, trace Poly, 1.7 g Sat); 25 mg Cholesterol; 19 g Carbohydrate; trace Fibre; 1 g Protein; 27 mg Sodium*

Pictured on page 143.

**tip**

When toasting nuts, seeds or coconut, cooking times will vary for each type of nut—so never toast them together. For small amounts, place ingredient in an ungreased frying pan. Heat on medium for 3 to 5 minutes, stirring often, until golden. For larger amounts, spread ingredient evenly in an ungreased shallow pan. Bake in a 350°F (175°C) oven for 5 to 10 minutes, stirring or shaking often, until golden.

# Lemon Smacks

*Such a light and lemony square.*

| | | |
|---|---|---|
| **BOTTOM LAYER** | | |
| **Egg yolks (large)** | **2** | **2** |
| **All-purpose flour** | **1 1/2 cups** | **375 mL** |
| **Brown sugar, packed** | **1/2 cup** | **125 mL** |
| **Butter (or hard margarine), softened** | **1/2 cup** | **125 mL** |
| **Baking powder** | **1 tsp.** | **5 mL** |
| **Salt** | **1/4 tsp.** | **1 mL** |
| **FILLING** | | |
| **Granulated sugar** | **1/2 cup** | **125 mL** |
| **Cornstarch** | **1/4 cup** | **60 mL** |
| **Large egg, fork-beaten** | **1** | **1** |
| **Water** | **1 cup** | **250 mL** |
| **Lemon juice** | **1/4 cup** | **60 mL** |
| **Salt** | **1/8 tsp.** | **0.5 mL** |
| **TOP LAYER** | | |
| **Egg whites (large), room temperature** | **2** | **2** |
| **Brown sugar, packed** | **1 cup** | **250 mL** |
| **Chopped walnuts (optional)** | **1/2 cup** | **125 mL** |

**Bottom Layer:** Mix all 6 ingredients in large bowl until crumbly. Press firmly into ungreased 9 x 9 inch (22 x 22 cm) pan.

**Filling:** Stir sugar and cornstarch in small saucepan. Add egg. Stir. Add next 3 ingredients. Stir well. Heat and stir on medium until boiling and thickened. Drop by teaspoonfuls, in dabs here and there, over bottom layer. Spread evenly.

**Top Layer:** Beat egg whites until frothy. Add brown sugar, 1/3 cup (75 mL) at a time, beating well after each addition until stiff peaks form. Fold in walnuts. Spread evenly over filling. Bake in 350°F (175°C) oven for about 25 minutes until starting to turn golden. Let stand in pan on wire rack until cool. Cuts into 36 squares.

***1 square:*** *94 Calories; 2.9 g Total Fat (0.8 g Mono, 0.1 g Poly, 1.7 g Sat); 24 mg Cholesterol; 17 g Carbohydrate; trace Fibre; 1 g Protein; 66 mg Sodium*

Pictured on page 143.

# Lemon Mardi Gras

*This is a cakey, one-layer square. Even with two beating times and one folding-in time, you can still have it in the oven in time to join the fun.*

| | | |
|---|---|---|
| Egg whites (large), room temperature | 2 | 2 |
| Granulated sugar | 1/2 cup | 125 mL |
| Granulated sugar | 1/2 cup | 125 mL |
| Butter (or hard margarine), softened | 1/4 cup | 60 mL |
| Lemon juice | 3 tbsp. | 50 mL |
| Egg yolks (large) | 2 | 2 |
| Grated lemon zest | 1 tsp. | 5 mL |
| All-purpose flour | 3/4 cup | 175 mL |
| Chopped walnuts | 1/3 cup | 75 mL |
| Baking powder | 1/2 tsp. | 2 mL |
| Salt | 1/4 tsp. | 1 mL |
| TOPPING | | |
| Granulated sugar | 1/4 cup | 60 mL |
| Lemon juice | 3 tbsp. | 50 mL |

Beat egg whites in medium bowl until frothy. Slowly add first amount of sugar, 1/4 cup (60 mL) at a time, beating well after each addition until stiff peaks form. Set aside.

Beat next 5 ingredients in separate, medium bowl until combined.

Add remaining 4 ingredients. Stir well. Fold in egg white mixture. Spread evenly in greased 8 x 8 inch (20 x 20 cm) pan. Bake in 400°F (205°C) oven for 20 to 25 minutes until wooden pick inserted in centre comes out clean. Cool slightly.

**Topping:** Combine sugar and lemon juice in small saucepan. Heat and stir on medium until sugar is dissolved. Drizzle over hot bottom layer. Let stand in pan on wire rack until cool. Cuts into 25 squares.

***1 square:*** *84 Calories; 3.2 g Total Fat (0.8 g Mono, 0.9 g Poly, 1.4 g Sat); 21 mg Cholesterol; 13 g Carbohydrate; trace Fibre; 1 g Protein; 52 mg Sodium*

Pictured on page 143.

# Butter Tart Bars

*These have a rich caramel taste and a soft, chewy texture.*

| | | |
|---|---|---|
| **BOTTOM LAYER** | | |
| **All-purpose flour** | **1 1/4 cups** | **300 mL** |
| **Butter (or hard margarine), softened** | **1/2 cup** | **125 mL** |
| **Brown sugar, packed** | **1/3 cup** | **75 mL** |
| **BUTTER TART LAYER** | | |
| **Large eggs** | **2** | **2** |
| **Brown sugar, packed** | **1 cup** | **250 mL** |
| **Raisins (or currants)** | **1 1/2 cups** | **375 mL** |
| **Chopped walnuts** | **1/2 cup** | **125 mL** |
| **Butter (or hard margarine), melted** | **1/4 cup** | **60 mL** |
| **All-purpose flour** | **1 tsp.** | **5 mL** |
| **Vanilla extract** | **1 tsp.** | **5 mL** |
| **Baking powder** | **1/2 tsp.** | **2 mL** |
| **Salt** | **1/4 tsp.** | **1 mL** |

**Bottom Layer:** Mix all 3 ingredients in medium bowl until crumbly. Press firmly into ungreased 9 x 9 inch (22 x 22 cm) pan. Bake in 350°F (175°C) oven for 15 minutes.

**Butter Tart Layer:** Beat eggs and brown sugar in large bowl. Add remaining 7 ingredients. Stir well. Spread evenly over bottom layer. Bake for about 20 minutes until light brown. Let stand in pan on wire rack until cool. Cuts into 36 squares.

***1 square:*** *115 Calories; 5.1 g Total Fat (1.1 g Mono, 0.9 g Poly, 2.6 g Sat); 22 mg Cholesterol; 17 g Carbohydrate; 1 g Fibre; 1 g Protein; 59 mg Sodium*

Pictured on page 143.

## Paré Pointer

*If you begin to feel nervous about eating all these squares, a good idea is to have the bathroom scale close to the sink counter so you can steady yourself while weighing by putting one hand on the counter.*

# Apricot Chews

*The finer the apricots are chopped, the better, as they give this square a lot of flavour.*

| | | |
|---|---|---|
| **BOTTOM LAYER** | | |
| **All-purpose flour** | **1 1/4 cups** | **300 mL** |
| **Brown sugar, packed** | **1/2 cup** | **125 mL** |
| **Butter (or hard margarine), softened** | **1/2 cup** | **125 mL** |
| **TOP LAYER** | | |
| **Large eggs** | **2** | **2** |
| **Flaked coconut** | **1 1/3 cups** | **325 mL** |
| **Can of sweetened condensed milk** | **11 oz.** | **300 mL** |
| **Finely chopped dried apricot** | **1 cup** | **250 mL** |
| **All-purpose flour** | **1/3 cup** | **75 mL** |
| **Baking powder** | **1 tsp.** | **5 mL** |

**Bottom Layer:** Mix all 3 ingredients in medium bowl until crumbly. Press firmly into ungreased 9 x 9 inch (22 x 22 cm) pan. Bake in 350°F (175°C) oven for 10 minutes.

**Top Layer:** Beat eggs in large bowl until frothy. Add remaining 5 ingredients. Stir well. Spread evenly over bottom layer. Bake for 25 to 30 minutes until firm. Let stand in pan on wire rack until cool. Cuts into 36 squares.

***1 square:** 113 Calories; 5.2 g Total Fat (0.7 g Mono, 0.1 g Poly, 3.7 g Sat); 21 mg Cholesterol; 15 g Carbohydrate; 1 g Fibre; 2 g Protein; 52 mg Sodium*

Pictured on page 143.

## *Paré Pointer*

*While waiting for a friend to meet you on a certain corner, and you buy snacks from a corner stand, that won't count on your diet. You are using the food as a legal device to avoid a loitering charge.*

# Raspberry Meringue

*A pretty treat to enhance any plate of goodies.*

| | | |
|---|---|---|
| **BOTTOM LAYER** | | |
| **Egg yolks (large)** | **2** | **2** |
| **All-purpose flour** | **1 1/2 cups** | **375 mL** |
| **Brown sugar, packed** | **3/4 cup** | **175 mL** |
| **Butter (or hard margarine), softened** | **1/2 cup** | **125 mL** |
| **Baking powder** | **2 tsp.** | **10 mL** |
| **FILLING** | | |
| **Raspberry jam, warmed** | **1 cup** | **250 mL** |
| **TOP LAYER** | | |
| **Egg whites (large), room temperature** | **2** | **2** |
| **Brown sugar, packed** | **3/4 cup** | **175 mL** |
| **Medium unsweetened coconut** | **1 cup** | **250 mL** |

**Bottom Layer:** Mix all 5 ingredients in medium bowl until crumbly. Press firmly into ungreased 9 x 9 inch (22 x 22 cm) pan.

**Filling:** Drop teaspoonfuls of jam, in dabs here and there, over bottom layer. Spread evenly.

**Top Layer:** Beat egg whites in medium bowl until frothy. Add brown sugar, 1/3 cup (75 mL) at a time, beating well after each addition until stiff peaks form. Fold in coconut. Spread evenly over filling. Bake in 350°F (175°C) oven for 25 to 30 minutes until golden. Let stand in pan on wire rack until cool. Cuts into 36 squares.

***1 square:** 114 Calories; 4.1 g Total Fat (0.8 g Mono, 0.2 g Poly, 3 g Sat); 18 mg Cholesterol; 19 g Carbohydrate; trace Fibre; 1 g Protein; 56 mg Sodium*

Pictured on page 144.

1. Sesame Squares, page 137
2. Brownies, page 136
3. Apricot Chews, page 141
4. Lemon Mardi Gras, page 139
5. Lemon Smacks, page 138
6. Caramel Toffee Squares, page 135
7. Butter Tart Bars, page 140
8. Butterscotch Toffee Bars, page 134

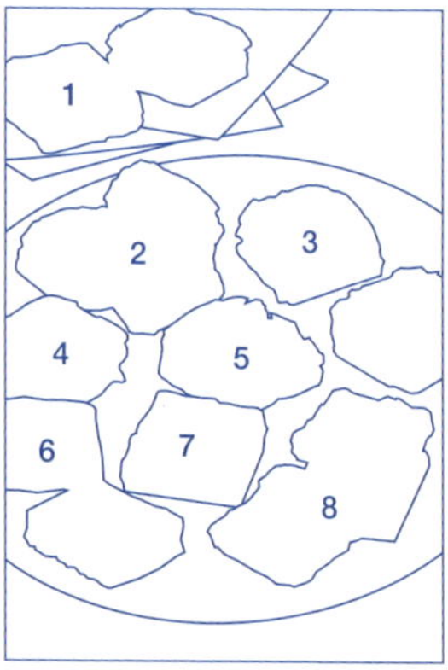

# Chocolate Smacks

*For a melt-in-your-mouth, lip-smacking snack, try this!*

| | | |
|---|---|---|
| **BOTTOM LAYER** | | |
| **Egg yolks (large)** | **2** | **2** |
| **All-purpose flour** | **1 1/4 cups** | **300 mL** |
| **Brown sugar, packed** | **1/2 cup** | **125 mL** |
| **Butter (or hard margarine), softened** | **1/2 cup** | **125 mL** |
| **Cocoa, sifted if lumpy** | **1/4 cup** | **60 mL** |
| **Baking powder** | **1 tsp.** | **5 mL** |
| **Salt** | **1/4 tsp.** | **1 mL** |
| **TOP LAYER** | | |
| **Egg whites (large), room temperature** | **2** | **2** |
| **Brown sugar, packed** | **1 cup** | **250 mL** |
| **Chopped walnuts** | **1 cup** | **250 mL** |
| **Cocoa, sifted if lumpy** | **2 tbsp.** | **30 mL** |

**Bottom Layer:** Mix all 7 ingredients in medium bowl until crumbly. Press firmly into ungreased 9 x 9 inch (22 x 22 cm) pan. Set aside.

**Top Layer:** Beat egg whites in separate medium bowl until frothy. Add brown sugar, 1/3 cup (75 mL) at a time, beating well after each addition until stiff peaks form.

Fold in walnuts and cocoa until no white streaks remain. Spread evenly over bottom layer. Bake in 350°F (175°C) oven for about 25 minutes until golden brown. Let stand in pan on wire rack until cool. Cuts into 36 squares.

***1 square:*** *100 Calories; 5.0 g Total Fat (1.1 g Mono, 1.7 g Poly, 1.9 g Sat); 18 mg Cholesterol; 13 g Carbohydrate; trace Fibre; 1 g Protein; 57 mg Sodium*

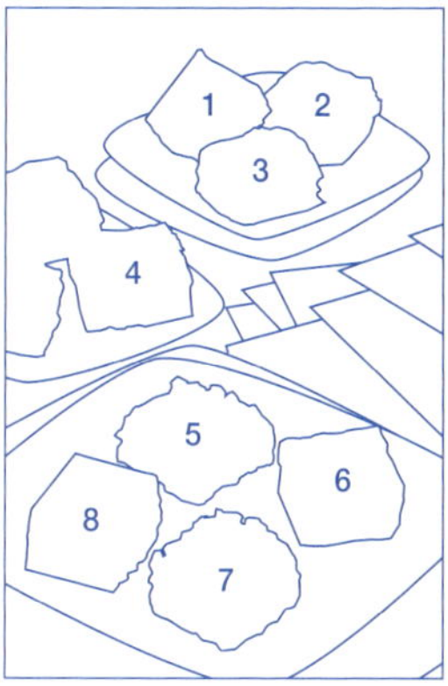


Pictured at left.


1. Almond Bars, page 151
2. Chocolate Smacks, above
3. Poppy Seed Squares, page 150
4. Walnut Bars, page 146
5. Raspberry Meringue, page 142
6. Raisin Spice Bars, page 148
7. Mystery Cake, page 149
8. Peanut Butter Chip Squares, page 147


Props courtesy of: Danesco Inc.

# Walnut Bars

*Crunchy walnuts and sweet coconut highlight this well-known bar.*

| | | |
|---|---|---|
| **BOTTOM LAYER** | | |
| All-purpose flour | 1 1/4 cups | 300 mL |
| Butter (or hard margarine), softened | 1/2 cup | 125 mL |
| Brown sugar, packed | 1/3 cup | 75 mL |
| **SECOND LAYER** | | |
| Large eggs | 2 | 2 |
| Vanilla extract | 1 tsp. | 5 mL |
| Brown sugar, packed | 1 1/4 cups | 300 mL |
| Chopped walnuts | 1 cup | 250 mL |
| Medium unsweetened coconut | 1/2 cup | 125 mL |
| All-purpose flour | 1 tsp. | 5 mL |
| Baking powder | 1/2 tsp. | 2 mL |
| Salt | 1/4 tsp. | 1 mL |
| **ICING** | | |
| Icing (confectioner's) sugar | 1 1/2 cups | 375 mL |
| Butter (or hard margarine), softened | 3 tbsp. | 50 mL |
| Milk | 1 1/2 tbsp. | 25 mL |
| Vanilla extract | 1/2 tsp. | 2 mL |

**Bottom Layer:** Mix all 3 ingredients in medium bowl until crumbly. Press firmly into ungreased 9 x 9 inch (22 x 22 cm) pan. Bake in 350°F (175°C) oven for 10 minutes.

**Second Layer:** Beat eggs with spoon in large bowl. Add next 7 ingredients in order given. Stir well. Spread evenly over bottom layer. Bake for about 25 minutes until light brown. Let stand in pan on wire rack until cool.

**Icing:** Beat all 4 ingredients in medium bowl until smooth, adding more milk or icing sugar as necessary until spreading consistency. Spread evenly over second layer. Cuts into 36 squares.

***1 square:*** *134 Calories; 6.6 g Total Fat (1.2 g Mono, 1.7 g Poly, 3.1 g Sat); 21 mg Cholesterol; 18 g Carbohydrate; trace Fibre; 1 g Protein; 57 mg Sodium*

Pictured on page 144.

**Variation:** Use 1/4 cup (60 mL) granulated sugar instead of brown sugar in bottom layer for a lighter-coloured base.

**Variation:** Sprinkle 1/3 cup (75 mL) crushed walnuts over icing.

# Peanut Butter Chip Squares

*It's hard to go wrong with creamy peanut butter and sweet chocolate.*

| | | |
|---|---|---|
| **BOTTOM LAYER** | | |
| Butter (or hard margarine) | 1/2 cup | 125 mL |
| Graham cracker crumbs | 1 1/4 cups | 300 mL |
| Brown sugar, packed | 1/2 cup | 125 mL |
| All-purpose flour | 1/3 cup | 75 mL |
| **SECOND LAYER** | | |
| Can of sweetened condensed milk | 11 oz. | 300 mL |
| Medium unsweetened coconut | 2 cups | 500 mL |
| **TOP LAYER** | | |
| Semi-sweet chocolate chips | 2 cups | 500 mL |
| Smooth peanut butter | 2 tbsp. | 30 mL |

**Bottom Layer:** Melt butter in medium saucepan on medium. Remove from heat. Stir in next 3 ingredients. Press firmly into ungreased 9 x 9 inch (22 x 22 cm) pan. Bake in 350°F (175°C) oven for 10 minutes.

**Second Layer:** Stir condensed milk into coconut in medium bowl (see Note). Immediately spread evenly over hot bottom layer. Bake for about 10 minutes until starting to turn golden.

**Top Layer:** Heat chocolate chips and peanut butter in small, heavy saucepan on lowest heat, stirring often until almost melted. Remove from heat. Stir until smooth. Spread evenly over second layer. Let stand in pan on wire rack until cool. Cuts into 36 squares.

***1 square:*** *157 Calories; 9.4 g Total Fat (1.8 g Mono, 0.3 g Poly, 6.2 g Sat); 9 mg Cholesterol; 18 g Carbohydrate; 1 g Fibre; 2 g Protein; 54 mg Sodium*

Pictured on page 144.

**Note:** Mix the coconut with condensed milk just before spreading so the coconut doesn't have time to soak up the milk, which makes it more difficult to spread.

### Paré Pointer

*If you are on a strict diet, eat all the maple syrup you can. Since it is a wood product you wouldn't count it any more than you would count toothpicks.*

# Raisin Spice Bars

*Similar to Raisin Squares, but adding warm spices creates a whole new taste.*

| | | |
|---|---|---|
| Raisins (or currants) | 1 cup | 250 mL |
| Brown sugar, packed | 1/2 cup | 125 mL |
| Water | 1/2 cup | 125 mL |
| Butter (or hard margarine) | 1/4 cup | 60 mL |
| Ground cinnamon | 1 tsp. | 5 mL |
| Salt | 1/2 tsp. | 2 mL |
| Ground cloves | 1/4 tsp. | 1 mL |
| Ground nutmeg | 1/4 tsp. | 1 mL |
| Water | 2 tsp. | 10 mL |
| Baking soda | 1/2 tsp. | 2 mL |
| All-purpose flour | 1 cup | 250 mL |
| Baking powder | 1 tsp. | 5 mL |
| ICING | | |
| Icing (confectioner's) sugar | 1 1/2 cups | 375 mL |
| Butter (or hard margarine), softened | 3 tbsp. | 50 mL |
| Lemon juice | 1 1/2 tbsp. | 25 mL |

Combine first 8 ingredients in large saucepan. Bring to a boil. Reduce heat to medium. Simmer for about 3 minutes, stirring occasionally until raisins are plump. Remove from heat.

Stir second amount of water into baking soda in small cup. Add to raisin mixture. Stir. Let stand until cool.

Add flour and baking powder. Stir well. Spread evenly in greased 8 x 8 inch (20 x 20 cm) pan. Bake in 350°F (175°C) oven for 25 to 30 minutes until set. Let stand in pan on wire rack until cool.

**Icing:** Beat all 3 ingredients in medium bowl until smooth, adding more lemon juice (see Note) or icing sugar as necessary until spreading consistency. Spread evenly over bottom layer. Cuts into 25 squares.

***1 square:** 111 Calories; 3.2 g Total Fat (0.8 g Mono, 0.1 g Poly, 2.0 g Sat); 8.4 mg Cholesterol; 20 g Carbohydrate; trace Fibre; 1 g Protein; 120 mg Sodium*

Pictured on page 144.

**Note:** If the icing is too lemony for your taste, replace some of the lemon juice with a little water.

*(continued on next page)*

**Variation:** Add a few drops of yellow food colouring to the icing for a nice yellow colour.

**Variation:** For a sweet touch of caramel flavour, replace the icing in this recipe with the icing from Caramel Slice, page 65.

# Mystery Cake

*A sweet and salty mix of dates and nuts is capped by a rich vanilla icing.*

| | | |
|---|---|---|
| **BOTTOM LAYER** | | |
| All-purpose flour | 2 cups | 500 mL |
| Butter (or hard margarine), softened | 1 cup | 250 mL |
| Granulated sugar | 1/2 cup | 125 mL |
| **SECOND LAYER** | | |
| Large eggs | 2 | 2 |
| Medium unsweetened coconut | 1 1/2 cups | 375 mL |
| Chopped pitted dates | 1 cup | 250 mL |
| Chopped walnuts | 1 cup | 250 mL |
| Brown sugar, packed | 1/2 cup | 125 mL |
| All-purpose flour | 2 tbsp. | 30 mL |
| Baking powder | 1/2 tsp. | 2 mL |
| **ICING** | | |
| Icing (confectioner's) sugar | 1 1/2 cups | 375 mL |
| Butter (or hard margarine), softened | 3 tbsp. | 50 mL |
| Milk | 1 1/2 tbsp. | 25 mL |
| Vanilla extract | 1/2 tsp. | 2 mL |

**Bottom Layer:** Mix all 3 ingredients in medium bowl until crumbly. Press firmly into ungreased 9 x 9 inch (22 x 22 cm) pan.

**Second Layer:** Beat eggs with spoon in large bowl. Add remaining 6 ingredients. Stir well. Spread evenly over bottom layer. Bake in 350°F (175°C) oven for about 30 minutes until golden brown. Let stand in pan on wire rack until cool.

**Icing:** Beat all 4 ingredients in medium bowl until smooth, adding more milk or icing sugar as necessary until spreading consistency. Spread evenly over second layer. Cuts into 36 squares.

***1 square:** 178 Calories; 10.4 g Total Fat (1.9 g Mono, 1.8 g Poly, 5.9 g Sat); 28 mg Cholesterol; 21 g Carbohydrate; 1 g Fibre; 2 g Protein; 57 mg Sodium*

Pictured on page 144.

# Poppy Seed Squares

*The caramel icing complements this square, but it's also very good without icing.*

| | | |
|---|---|---|
| Poppy seeds | 1/2 cup | 125 mL |
| Milk | 2 tbsp. | 30 mL |
| All-purpose flour | 1 3/4 cups | 425 mL |
| Granulated sugar | 1 1/4 cups | 300 mL |
| Baking powder | 1 tsp. | 5 mL |
| Salt | 1/2 tsp. | 2 mL |
| Baking soda | 1/4 tsp. | 1 mL |
| Butter (or hard margarine), melted | 1/2 cup | 125 mL |
| Liquid honey | 1/3 cup | 75 mL |
| Vanilla extract | 1 tsp. | 5 mL |
| Large eggs | 2 | 2 |
| Medium unsweetened coconut | 1 cup | 250 mL |
| ICING | | |
| Brown sugar, packed | 3/4 cup | 175 mL |
| Butter (or hard margarine) | 1/4 cup | 60 mL |
| Milk | 2 tbsp. | 30 mL |
| Icing (confectioner's) sugar | 1 1/2 cups | 375 mL |

Stir poppy seeds into milk in small cup. Let stand for 10 minutes.

Combine next 5 ingredients in large bowl. Make a well in centre.

Add next 4 ingredients. Beat well.

Add coconut and poppy seed mixture. Spread evenly in greased 9 x 13 inch (22 x 33 cm) pan. Bake in 350°F (175°C) oven for 25 to 30 minutes until wooden pick inserted in centre comes out clean. Let stand in pan on wire rack until cool.

**Icing:** Combine first 3 ingredients in medium saucepan. Heat and stir on medium until melted. Bring to a boil. Reduce heat to medium-low. Simmer, uncovered, for 2 minutes, stirring occasionally. Cool for about 30 minutes until lukewarm.

Add icing sugar. Beat until light and creamy, adding more milk or icing sugar as necessary until spreading consistency. Spread evenly over bottom layer. Cuts into 54 squares.

***1 square:*** *105 Calories; 4.3 g Total Fat (0.7 g Mono, 0.1 g Poly, 2.5 g Sat); 15 mg Cholesterol; 16 g Carbohydrate; trace Fibre; 1 g Protein; 60 mg Sodium*

Pictured on page 144.

# Almond Bars

*The sweet warmth of almonds and cinnamon make this a festive treat.*

| | | |
|---|---|---|
| **BOTTOM LAYER** | | |
| **All-purpose flour** | **1 1/2 cups** | **375 mL** |
| **Butter (or hard margarine), softened** | **2/3 cup** | **150 mL** |
| **Granulated sugar** | **6 tbsp.** | **100 mL** |
| **SECOND LAYER** | | |
| **Whipping cream** | **1/2 cup** | **125 mL** |
| **Egg yolk (large), fork-beaten** | **1** | **1** |
| **Ground almonds** | **1/2 cup** | **125 mL** |
| **Brown sugar, packed** | **1 tbsp.** | **15 mL** |
| **Ground cinnamon** | **1 tsp.** | **5 mL** |
| **LEMON GLAZE** | | |
| **Lemon juice** | **1 tbsp.** | **15 mL** |
| **Icing (confectioner's) sugar** | **1/2 cup** | **125 mL** |

**Bottom Layer:** Mix all 3 ingredients in medium bowl until crumbly. Press firmly into ungreased 8 x 8 inch (20 x 20 cm) pan. Bake in 325°F (160°C) oven for 10 minutes. Cool slightly.

**Second Layer:** Whip cream in small bowl until soft peaks form. Fold in next 4 ingredients. Spread evenly over bottom layer. Bake for about 40 minutes until golden. Let stand in pan on wire rack until cool.

**Lemon Glaze:** Stir lemon juice into icing sugar in small bowl, adding more lemon juice or icing sugar as necessary until barely pourable consistency. Spread evenly over second layer. Let stand in pan until glaze is set. Cuts into 25 squares.

***1 square:*** *121 Calories; 7.9 g Total Fat (2.5 g Mono, 0.5 g Poly, 4.3 g Sat); 28 mg Cholesterol; 12 g Carbohydrate; trace Fibre; 1 g Protein; 37 mg Sodium*

Pictured on page 144.

## Paré Pointer

*Don't worry if you visit a friend in the hospital and sample his chocolates. Just read the card—it states very clearly that it's all intended for him.*

# Measurement Tables

Throughout this book measurements are given in Conventional and Metric measure. To compensate for differences between the two measurements due to rounding, a full metric measure is not always used. The cup used is the standard 8 fluid ounce. Temperature is given in degrees Fahrenheit and Celsius. Baking pan measurements are in inches and centimetres as well as quarts and litres. An exact metric conversion is given below as well as the working equivalent (Metric Standard Measure).

## Oven Temperatures

| Fahrenheit (°F) | Celsius (°C) |
|---|---|
| 175° | 80° |
| 200° | 95° |
| 225° | 110° |
| 250° | 120° |
| 275° | 140° |
| 300° | 150° |
| 325° | 160° |
| 350° | 175° |
| 375° | 190° |
| 400° | 205° |
| 425° | 220° |
| 450° | 230° |
| 475° | 240° |
| 500° | 260° |

## Pans

| Conventional Inches | Metric Centimetres |
|---|---|
| 8x8 inch | 20x20 cm |
| 9x9 inch | 22x22 cm |
| 9x13 inch | 22x33 cm |
| 10x15 inch | 25x38 cm |
| 11x17 inch | 28x43 cm |
| 8x2 inch round | 20x5 cm |
| 9x2 inch round | 22x5 cm |
| 10x4 1/2 inch tube | 25x11 cm |
| 8x4x3 inch loaf | 20x10x7.5 cm |
| 9x5x3 inch loaf | 22x12.5x7.5 cm |

## Spoons

| Conventional Measure | Metric Exact Conversion Millilitre (mL) | Metric Standard Measure Millilitre (mL) |
|---|---|---|
| 1/8 teaspoon (tsp.) | 0.6 mL | 0.5 mL |
| 1/4 teaspoon (tsp.) | 1.2 mL | 1 mL |
| 1/2 teaspoon (tsp.) | 2.4 mL | 2 mL |
| 1 teaspoon (tsp.) | 4.7 mL | 5 mL |
| 2 teaspoons (tsp.) | 9.4 mL | 10 mL |
| 1 tablespoon (tbsp.) | 14.2 mL | 15 mL |

## Cups

| Conventional Measure | Metric Exact Conversion Millilitre (mL) | Metric Standard Measure Millilitre (mL) |
|---|---|---|
| 1/4 cup (4 tbsp.) | 56.8 mL | 60 mL |
| 1/3 cup (5 1/3 tbsp.) | 75.6 mL | 75 mL |
| 1/2 cup (8 tbsp.) | 113.7 mL | 125 mL |
| 2/3 cup (10 2/3 tbsp.) | 151.2 mL | 150 mL |
| 3/4 cup (12 tbsp.) | 170.5 mL | 175 mL |
| 1 cup (16 tbsp.) | 227.3 mL | 250 mL |
| 4 1/2 cups | 1022.9 mL | 1000 mL (1 L) |

## Dry Measurements

| Conventional Measure Ounces (oz.) | Metric Exact Conversion Grams (g) | Metric Standard Measure Grams (g) |
|---|---|---|
| 1 oz. | 28.3 g | 28 g |
| 2 oz. | 56.7 g | 57 g |
| 3 oz. | 85.0 g | 85 g |
| 4 oz. | 113.4 g | 125 g |
| 5 oz. | 141.7 g | 140 g |
| 6 oz. | 170.1 g | 170 g |
| 7 oz. | 198.4 g | 200 g |
| 8 oz. | 226.8 g | 250 g |
| 16 oz. | 453.6 g | 500 g |
| 32 oz. | 907.2 g | 1000 g (1 kg) |

## Casseroles

| CANADA & BRITAIN | | UNITED STATES | |
|---|---|---|---|
| Standard Size Casserole | Exact Metric Measure | Standard Size Casserole | Exact Metric Measure |
| 1 qt. (5 cups) | 1.13 L | 1 qt. (4 cups) | 900 mL |
| 1 1/2 qts. (7 1/2 cups) | 1.69 L | 1 1/2 qts. (6 cups) | 1.35 L |
| 2 qts. (10 cups) | 2.25 L | 2 qts. (8 cups) | 1.8 L |
| 2 1/2 qts. (12 1/2 cups) | 2.81 L | 2 1/2 qts. (10 cups) | 2.25 L |
| 3 qts. (15 cups) | 3.38 L | 3 qts. (12 cups) | 2.7 L |
| 4 qts. (20 cups) | 4.5 L | 4 qts. (16 cups) | 3.6 L |
| 5 qts. (25 cups) | 5.63 L | 5 qts. (20 cups) | 4.5 L |

# Recipe Index

## D



## E



## F

## N



## O



## P



## Q



## R

## S



## T



## V



## W

## Recipe Notes

# Recipe Notes

# The Company's Coming Story

Jean Paré (pronounced "jeen PAIR-ee") grew up understanding that the combination of family, friends and home cooking is the best recipe for a good life. From her mother, she learned to appreciate good cooking, while her father praised even her earliest attempts in the kitchen. When Jean left home, she took with her a love of cooking, many family recipes and an intriguing desire to read cookbooks as if they were novels!

*"Never share a recipe you wouldn't use yourself."*

When her four children had all reached school age, Jean volunteered to cater the 50th anniversary celebration of the Vermilion School of Agriculture, now Lakeland College, in Alberta, Canada. Working out of her home, Jean prepared a dinner for more than 1,000 people, launching a flourishing catering operation that continued for over 18 years. During that time, she had countless opportunities to test new ideas with immediate feedback—resulting in empty plates and contented customers! Whether preparing cocktail sandwiches for a house party or serving a hot meal for 1,500 people, Jean Paré earned a reputation for great food, courteous service and reasonable prices.

As requests for her recipes increased, Jean was often asked the question, "Why don't you write a cookbook?" Jean responded by teaming up with her son, Grant Lovig, in the fall of 1980 to form Company's Coming Publishing Limited. The publication of *150 Delicious Squares* on April 14, 1981 marked the debut of what would soon become one of the world's most popular cookbook series.

The company has grown since those early days when Jean worked from a spare bedroom in her home. Today, she continues to write recipes while working closely with the staff of the Recipe Factory, as the Company's Coming test kitchen is affectionately known. There she fills the role of mentor, assisting with the development of recipes people most want to use for everyday cooking and easy entertaining. Every Company's Coming recipe is *kitchen-tested* before it is approved for publication.

Jean's daughter, Gail Lovig, is responsible for marketing and distribution, leading a team that includes sales personnel located in major cities across Canada. Company's Coming cookbooks are distributed in Canada, the United States, Australia and other world markets. Bestsellers many times over in English, Company's Coming cookbooks have also been published in French and Spanish.

Familiar and trusted in home kitchens around the world, Company's Coming cookbooks are offered in a variety of formats. Highly regarded as kitchen workbooks, the softcover Original Series, with its lay-flat plastic comb binding, is still a favourite among readers.

Jean Paré's approach to cooking has always called for *quick and easy recipes* using *everyday ingredients.* That view has served her well. The recipient of many awards, including the Queen Elizabeth Golden Jubilee Medal, Jean was appointed Member of the Order of Canada, her country's highest lifetime achievement honour.

Jean continues to gain new supporters by adhering to what she calls The Golden Rule of Cooking: *Never share a recipe you wouldn't use yourself.* It's an approach that has worked—*millions of times over!*